HAUNTED PHILADELPHIA

Famous Phantoms, Sinister Sites, and Lingering Legends

Darcy Oordt

Globe
Pequot

Guilford, Connecticut

Globe
Pequot

An imprint of Rowman & Littlefield

Distributed by NATIONAL BOOK NETWORK

Copyright © 2015 by Rowman & Littlefield

British Library Cataloguing in Publication Information Available

Library of Congress Cataloging-in-Publication Data Available

ISBN 978-1-4930-1579-5 (paperback)
ISBN 978-1-4930-1580-1 (e-book)

CONTENTS

ACKNOWLEDGMENTS

I likely never would have written this book had it not been for my agent, Regina Ryan. She took me on when I was an unpublished author and stuck with me when I had nothing to write. Thank you. I must also thank Maggie Moore, who pushes me to continue writing when life gets in the way. We are family in a way that is stronger than birth would have made us.

I also want to thank my father, who has supported my less-than-lucrative writing career choice, and my brother, who first exposed me to ghosts when we watched *Poltergeist* huddled together under a blanket on the family room couch. I also want to thank Perry and my other coworkers at Broad Street Media for giving me the time needed to write. Thanks also to everyone who answered my questions and gave interviews for this book.

Finally, I want to thank my editor, Erin Turner, for answering all my questions and guiding me without taking away my voice. Also thanks to Courtney Oppel, who fixed all my grammatical mistakes and made me look like a better writer, and Staci Zacharski for somehow making this all fit. I also want to thank everyone else at Globe Pequot who participated in making this book possible. I can't name you here because I had to write this section before the book was done. You all deserve credit for dealing with me. (I know me, and I can be hard to work with.)

I dedicate this book to all the people who lived and died to make this book possible. We can forget that each ghost represents a person who once lived, had a family, and often died too soon. I hope by telling your story that I honor that life and memorialize your passing.

INTRODUCTION

If you ask someone what Philly is best known for, their answer will likely reflect their interests. A historian will tell you that it was where our country's government was founded. Art lovers may mention that it has one of the largest art museums or the largest public art program that includes more than two thousand outdoor murals. Movie fans will tell you it's Rocky Balboa's hometown and where the movies *Mannequin* and *Sixth Sense* were filmed. Food lovers can tell you that the cheesesteak, hoagie, soft pretzel, and water ice were established in Philadelphia. Shopaholics know Philadelphia as being the home of the nation's first department store, Wanamaker's. Sports lovers know Philadelphia as the home of eight professional sports teams.

Ghost enthusiasts are likely to mention Eastern State Penitentiary or Fort Mifflin, the two most famous haunted locations in Philadelphia. Nearly every ghost reality show that has come to Philadelphia has visited one of those two locations, if not both of them. But there is a world of the paranormal that exists beyond those two sites.

As you page through this book, you will notice that it is divided into geographical sections and includes addresses so you can visit the locations if you desire. Within those sections, I tried to group stories into chapters that made sense either geographically or by theme.

Whenever I told people that I was writing a book about Philadelphia ghosts, they inevitably asked me which story was my favorite. Truthfully, I don't have a favorite story, but I do have several ghosts that I have come to love.

I worked as a guide for a ghost tour for several years. As a result I established friendships with several ghosts on the tour. They often appeared during my tour and interacted with me and my tour. They often drained batteries in phones and cameras. When I started to warn people in my tour group, the ghosts switched tactics. They still drained batteries, but then they would fill them back up. Repeatedly. That way they could let me know they were there, but still let people have the opportunity to take pictures.

They did other things as well. My favorite event occurred on the way to the tour as I was listening to Bon Jovi's "Wanted Dead or Alive." My radio suddenly lost its signal as I drove past the building they haunted. I didn't get my radio back until after I passed by. I had satellite radio and had never lost the signal there before. I share this because my experiences taught me that ghosts have personalities and are as "real" as we are.

But as much as I believe in ghosts, I consider myself a skeptical believer. That means I always look for possible explanations before I consider an event as caused by a true "ghost." For example, going back to my story with the radio, had I wanted to prove it truly was related to "ghosts" I would have called and found out if they had any outages at the time of my experience. It's possible that one of the few times I was listening to a song about the "dead" while driving by a haunted location the system lost its signal. And I admit that had it happened any other time or place, I would have written it off as "solar flares" or some other such thing.

Such is the world of the paranormal. It is filled with things that we can't explain—sometimes because we can find no explanation, other times because we don't look for one.

As you read this book, you will find that the stories are grouped by geographical location in all but a few cases. Hopefully, you'll find the time to visit the locations that are open to the public.

The last section of the book talks about Philadelphia cemeteries. Originally, I planned on including a list of cemeteries located in Philadelphia. But as I compiled the list I found that quite a few of them had been relocated. Then I discovered that some cemeteries which everyone thought had been moved hadn't been moved at all. Just like in the movie *Poltergeist*, people moved the gravestones but left the bodies and then built over them.

The list started out small, with just five or six locations. As I researched them, I started adding names to my list. Eventually I had a list of over 100 locations. Included in this book are the ones I could verify through either historical documents or atlases. As a ghost enthusiast, you may want to check them out and see if any spirits linger.

Part One:

OLD CITY AND INDEPENDENCE NATIONAL HISTORIC PARK

Old City is an area located inside Center City roughly bounded in the north by Wood and Callowhill Streets, by Walnut and Chestnut Streets in the south, Independence Park to the west, and the Delaware River to the east. The first Europeans settled here in 1676.

Bordering Old City is Independence National Historic Park, which lies on fifty-five acres in the center of Philadelphia. Due to the high number of historical landmarks, people refer to it as "America's most historic square mile." But it should be called America's most historic haunted square mile.

The ghosts are as old and famous as the buildings they haunt, which makes any ghost tour a lesson in American history. Benjamin Franklin, Betsy Ross, Bishop White, Benjamin Rush, Alexander Hamilton, and even the entire First Continental Congress all haunt their former stomping grounds.

Chapter 1

The Many Ghosts of Ben Franklin

To the rest of the world, Benjamin Franklin died in 1793, but Philadelphians know the truth. Although he left his physical body, he never left the city he loved and called home. Even those who claim not to believe in ghosts have to admit that Franklin's spirit lingers in the city. Whether that ghost is throwing pennies, pinching women, or walking down the streets of Philly wearing a toga, it always makes an impression.

Of all the Founding Fathers, Benjamin Franklin is particularly unique. Although he never served in the military, his influence and skills helped win the Revolutionary War and shape the foundation of the United States. He is the only Founding Father to have signed the Declaration of Independence, the Treaty of Alliance with France, The Treaty of Paris establishing peace with Great Britain, and the U.S. Constitution. He also wrote and signed the Petition from the Pennsylvania Society of the Abolition of Slavery in 1790.

Benjamin Franklin also helped found the first lending library, first liberal arts academy, first public hospital, and the first volunteer fire department in the United States. He was also an inventor, musician, scientist, cartographer, author, and publisher. All of these things he achieved with a minimal formal education.

Franklin is also notorious for being a womanizer, a reputation he promoted during the later years of his life. However, historians disagree about how much of his reputation was deserved. Claude-Anne Lope perhaps described him best in a 2003 *Time* magazine article by saying he was the "master of what the French call *amitie amoureuse*." This translates to "amorous friendship" which means Franklin flirted, wrote love letters, and shared embraces with numerous women but not necessarily anything more intimate.

The multifaceted nature of Ben Franklin continues. It seems only natural that a man who dabbled in a variety of interests would ensure that his legacy appealed to everyone, including ghost lovers. A man like Franklin cannot be satisfied with haunting just one location in Philadelphia. He haunts several locations, including the streets of Philadelphia. So if you are in the city and see a man resembling Franklin, don't discount it as a reenactor. It may be the great man himself!

CHRIST CHURCH BURIAL GROUND
20 NORTH AMERICAN STREET

Christ Church Burial Ground was established in 1719 when the Christ Church purchased two acres on (what was then) the edge of town. It is still an active burial ground, and more than 4,000 people have been buried there in its 300-year history. Sadly, only 1,500 of the original gravestones remain, many of which have had their inscriptions erased by erosion.

One gravestone still clearly visible is Benjamin Franklin's. Franklin was buried next to his wife in the northwest corner of the cemetery. Two thousand mourners attended his funeral, and his grave soon became a frequent visiting spot. In 1858, an opening in the cemetery's brick wall was put in at the bequest of Franklin's descendants. That way people would have constant access to Franklin's grave, even after the cemetery was closed.

The Philly custom is to throw a penny onto Franklin's grave for luck and in honor of Franklin. The custom came about because many people quote him as having said, "A penny saved is a penny earned." But he didn't. Franklin did include something similar in the preface to his 1758 almanac: "A penny saved is a penny got," which is an old English proverb.

And it might seem strange to Franklin that he is being honored by people throwing away pennies, when he was known for telling people to save their pennies. But the Christ Church doesn't mind. They sweep up the pennies and use them toward preserving the cemetery. In 2004, they collected $750. That's 75,000 pennies.

But Franklin might feel pennies are a little stingy. His face is on the $100 bill, not the penny. Why not throw those instead? Since no one has started that trend, Franklin uses other methods to collect money. People have reported loose change vanishing out of their pockets while visiting Franklin's grave.

Franklin's ghost is also blamed for throwing money back at people. In July 1976 a registered nurse, Joanna Flynn, reported feeling something hit her neck and then noticing a penny rolling toward the curb in front of her. She turned around, but didn't see anyone, so she ignored it. Until a second penny struck her. According to Flynn, "Anger filled me, and I was ready to give this wise guy a good piece of my mind, but there was absolutely no one around." Maybe

Franklin was upset that she hadn't thrown a penny or that she was ignoring him.

Oh, and women should take note. Women report being goosed here—something that Franklin's ghost also does down the street at Library Hall.

AMERICAN PHILOSOPHICAL SOCIETY'S LIBRARY HALL
105 SOUTH FIFTH STREET

Ben Franklin's spirit is felt across Philadelphia, but he is only seen at places to which he had a strong connection during his life. Why then would his ghost frequent Library Hall, which was built in the 1950s?

Library Hall was originally built in 1789 or 1790 as the new headquarters for the Library Company of Philadelphia (LCP). Ben Franklin founded LCP in 1731 as a subscription library supported by its shareholders, a tradition which continues to this day. Since Franklin died in 1790, he would not have spent any real time in this building, at least not while he was alive.

Only after his death did he start hanging around the building. A cleaning lady reported seeing Franklin's ghost often in the mid-1880s. Almost every morning while she cleaned the building she would see a man dressed in seventeenth-century clothing wandering through the library whispering to himself. He would move books around, even climbing ladders to reach them. Other times he paced back and forth or leaned over a table to study some papers.

No problems arose from the ghost until one day in 1884 when Franklin rushed past and knocked the woman over. The woman, upset the ghost didn't stop to apologize, chased

Should Be Haunted: Franklin's Ghost House

317 Chestnut Street

With Franklin's ghost wandering around Philadelphia, the words "Franklin's ghost house" naturally invoke the idea of where his spirit spends its leisure time, as if Franklin's ghost gets up, goes to Library Hall, and stops by the Christ Church Burial Ground and City Tavern before returning to his ghost house.

In reality, the ghost house is composed of two structures made of tubular steel that suggest where Franklin's home and print shop once stood. The original house and print shop built by Franklin were torn down in 1812 by his heirs. The site was acquired by the National Park Service in the 1950s, but years of construction on the site had destroyed almost all traces of it.

Without any historical documentation about the house, it became impossible to recreate the buildings as had been hoped. Instead, architects Robert Venturi and John Rauch, along with Denise Brown, designed the "hollow" compromise for the Bicentennial in 1976 to suggest where the house and print shop once stood. No ghosts are included, but a museum exists underneath.

after him. When she caught up to him, she lectured him on how a gentleman should behave. Finally, Franklin turned around, folded his arms, and bowed an apology to her. Afterwards, the ghost cautiously avoided rooms being cleaned until she was through, occasionally peeking around the corner to check whether she was finished.

Sightings of Franklin stopped after the building was demolished in 1887 to make way for the Drexel & Company Building. The building might have been forgotten until the American Philosophical Society decided to build a library in 1958 and recreated the façade of the original building. The action not only brought back Library Hall, it brought back Franklin's ghost.

People still report seeing Franklin's ghostly figure carrying books through the building. And it appears Franklin forgot the lecture he received about how a gentleman should behave, since women report feeling pinched by an unseen hand (and Franklin was a notorious flirt).

Recently, an employee who works in the building reported that a visitor showed her a photo of the building taken using an iPhone on a recent tour. In one of the windows appeared a figure that resembled Franklin, which is particularly odd since the library was closed when the picture was taken and no one should have been inside.

According to Franklin's autobiography, he believed that "Libraries have improved the general Conversation of Americans, made the common Tradesmen and Farmers as intelligent as most Gentlemen from other Countries." Perhaps he feels this improvement should continue even after death.

BEN FRANKLIN'S STATUE

Several Benjamin Franklin statues can be found across the city. But none is as notorious as the one found in the front of Library Hall, which features Franklin dressed in a toga. Surprisingly, Franklin requested the strange apparel. He felt it would explain how he viewed himself: as an heir to a republic like Rome or Athens.

What makes this statue of Franklin especially unique are the reports of it leaving its pedestal. Shortly after Franklin died, people reported seeing the statue walking the streets of Philadelphia. Some report seeing the statue making its way toward Franklin's house, as the real Franklin did on so many occasions. Others report seeing the statue dancing or skipping along Philadelphia streets. There are even claims that it visits local pubs, like City Tavern.

Chapter 2

Famous Revolutionary Houses

Three famous Revolutionary figures, several former employees, and even a cat are among the ghosts that haunt the former houses of Betsy Ross, Bishop White, and Benjamin Rush. Although only two houses remain, all three areas are open to the public and welcome visitors.

BETSY ROSS HOUSE
239 ARCH STREET

Long hours are expected when you are the director of a 275-year-old house that receives more than a quarter of a million visitors each year. It wasn't uncommon to find the former director of the Betsy Ross house working late in her attic office. One night, she was typing on her computer long after the doors closed when she felt a hand grasp her shoulder. She turned to see who else was working late and found the room empty.

At that moment, she recalled a story about her predecessor climbing onto the flagpole outside the office window after becoming frightened by something experienced in the attic. What she experienced is unknown because she refused to speak about it.

Betsy Ross could be considered the Kim Kardashian of her era: both are famous, both created scandals, and there's debate about what either has actually contributed to the American culture. Born Elizabeth Griscom in 1752, Betsy Ross was the eighth of seventeen children. She attended a Quaker school and eventually apprenticed with a local upholsterer. While there, she fell in love with another young apprentice, John Ross. Despite the scandal of marrying someone outside the Quaker religion, Betsy married John in 1772. Together they started their own upholstery business, which Betsy continued to run after John died in a gunpowder explosion in 1776, during the start of the American Revolution.

Despite working day and night in her shop, Betsy managed to meet and marry Joseph Ashburn in 1777. Tragically, Joseph died in 1782 in prison after the British captured his ship. Before passing away, Joseph asked a fellow prison mate, John Claypoole, to deliver his last words back to his beloved wife. John honored these wishes and eventually fell in love with the twice-widowed shop owner. The two married in 1783. This marriage lasted thirty-four years until John passed away in 1817. Elizabeth "Betsy" Griscom Ross Ashburn Claypoole would live another nine years before passing away at age eighty-four.

While Betsy lived an incredible life and accomplished much during her time, no historical proof exists that she did what she is most famous for: sewing the first American flag. Documents from 1877 show that she was paid to make "ship's colours." But no historical evidence exists that prove Betsy created "Old Glory" for George Washington in June 1776, other than the story told by her grandson to *Harper's Weekly* in 1873.

There's also some dispute whether Betsy ever lived at the slender red-bricked building that was built in 1740 and bears her name. Betsy may have rented several rooms in the house from 1775 to 1779, when she is believed to have created the famous first flag. Surviving members of Betsy's family didn't declare 239 Arch Street as "the" house until 1876. But, again, no evidence exists that she ever resided there.

But even if she didn't live there or make the first flag, she is at least buried there. Probably. Possibly. Well, you know how tricky moving can be. It doesn't always work out the way you planned.

After her death in 1836, she was buried at the Free Quaker Burial Ground on South Fifth Street next to her third husband. Then, in 1856, family members exhumed the pair and moved them to the family plot in Mount Moriah Cemetery. They remained there until 1975, when city officials decided to move Betsy's body to a more historically significant spot.

On December 15, 1975, a group of grave diggers supervised by archaeologist Dr. Allan Mann began digging underneath Betsy's headstone . . . and digging . . . and digging. They dug for four hours, but all they found was dirt. So they started digging in other places around the plot until they discovered a coffin a few feet away. But it turned out to be the body of either Betsy's grandson or great-grandson. The grave diggers returned and dug for several more hours until finally, at the opposite end of the family plot, they uncovered bones that Mann determined were Betsy's.

Mann was likely under considerable pressure from city officials eager to reinter Betsy Ross's bones for the country's Bicentennial. Several newspapers quote Mann as saying that he was nervous about "getting blamed for losing Betsy Ross." Mann speculated that the acidic soil could have erased all traces of the beloved seamstress or she might never have been moved in the first place.

Exactly whose bones were taken can be debated, but they were declared to be those of John Claypoole and Betsy Ross when they were reinterred in the garden next to the Betsy Ross house.

Charles H. Weisgerber was an artist who painted an enormous picture of three patriots visiting Ross. He also formed the Betsy Ross Memorial Association designed to preserve the house and moved into the building, where he lived as caretaker for thirty-six years. He was such a fanboy of Betsy that he named his son Vexil Domus, Latin for "flag house." The association was responsible for buying and demolishing several houses next to the "Ross" house in the 1930s to create a small park—an action that, some historians argue, probably destroyed the real house Ross lived in because street numbers have changed. Charles died in the attic in 1931. The attic is now the director's office and remains a primary location of ghostly experiences.

But the hauntings are not limited to the attic. Almost every room in the house has reported ghostly activity. On the second floor, a visiting psychic claimed to have seen Betsy Ross sitting on the end of the bed weeping. While in the parlor, where supposedly the famous meeting between Ross and George Washington took place, visitors have reported seeing disembodied shadows moving around as well as voices.

Disembodied voices are often heard in the basement. Although they rarely speak loud enough to be heard, a curator distinctly heard a man's voice say, "Pardon me." Perhaps it was Charles H. Weisgerber making apologies to his predecessor? On another occasion, an admission staff member, Elaine, was sitting in the basement by herself when she heard voices and movement coming from another part of the

room, although she was alone. The feeling of being watched is also reported here.

Even the gift shop has not escaped paranormal activity, although technically it's next door to the house. In 1980, two security guards got into a clash in the basement of the gift shop. One security guard shot the other guard three times and then left him in the gift shop basement overnight to die. Since then, staff members have heard footsteps and voices coming from here. In 2008, several staff members heard boxes being moved around in the loft above the gift shop, although no one was nearby.

In December 2008, The Atlantic Paranormal Society (TAPS) conducted an investigation for their TV show *Ghost Hunters*. While at the site, Grant Wilson and Jason Hawes heard voices in the attic as well as footsteps walking above them while they were in the basement.

BISHOP WHITE HOUSE
309 WALNUT STREET

Don't judge a book by its cover or a house by its exterior. On the outside, the Bishop White House looks almost cheery with its red brick and antique white shutters. But inside this Georgian-style row house is a different story, which earned it the title as the creepiest and most haunted house in Independence Park by park rangers and visitors. Few people journey into the house alone, especially at night, because of an overwhelming feeling of uneasiness commonly experienced in the house.

Rev. Dr. William White built the house in 1787. He chose a location midway between the two churches he served, Christ Church and St. Peter's Church. Bishop White is known as the spiritual advisor for our nation's founders and became the first bishop of the Protestant Episcopal Church of America. He was so committed to his ministry that he refused to flee the city during the Yellow Fever outbreaks in 1790 as most other people of his wealth and status did. Bishop White never contracted the deadly disease, thought in part due to his heavy cigar smoking, which kept away the mosquitos that carried the disease. (One of the first times smoking saved someone's life.) Some of his staff were not as lucky.

A coachman known only as John lived behind the house and died of the disease. John and Bishop White were friends and companions, despite their difference in class, status, and race—John was a free African American. Benjamin Rush, a doctor and neighbor, wrote in a letter to his wife that Mrs. Boggs was knocking on the door and he needed to tend a patient next door. That patient was John.

Mrs. Boggs was the main cook in the house in the late 1700s. Although the Whites had a number of staff, she and John are the only two servants mentioned by name in letters written by the White family, showing that she was important to the family. She lived directly above the kitchen with several other servants. Exactly when or how she died is unclear.

John may be one of the "shadowy shapes" that people report seeing moving through the house. No one has mentioned seeing John in the house, but there have been sightings of Mrs. Boggs in the kitchen and first floor of the house.

When standing outside the building, take particular note of the windows on the third floor. People often see a tall, thin, grim-faced man peering out the window of the library. Some believe the ghost is Bishop White because he died in that room. White's bedroom, however, was located on the second floor of the house. Since White died at age eight-five after a lengthy illness, he probably died in his own bedroom.

Still, White's death affected the house and caused the dark mood currently associated with the house. According to his obituary, which appeared in various newspapers in July 1836, Bishop White "passed away from life as he passed through it—calm and serene, and full of edification. . . . It was strange that . . . at his death there should have been a general gloom [because] a great and good man had been taken away, and it was seemly that the people should take it to heart." The gloomy feeling caused by White's death never left the house.

White's death wasn't the first death here. Five of Bishop White's children died before reaching adulthood. His wife, Mary, also died in the house in 1797. Many speculate that the house itself may have caused these deaths, or rather a feature in the house: an indoor bathroom.

Plumbing didn't exist then. Toilet waste was removed and disposed into an open gully in the basement, next to where the household drinking water came from. This proximity could have contaminated the drinking water and caused some of the deaths in the house.

The gully emptied out into Dock Creek, which ran through the backyards of several houses, including Bishop White's. The creek was polluted by human waste, along with remains from a nearby slaughterhouse, and was likely a breeding ground for many of the mosquitos that spread yellow fever in the 1790s.

One strange sighting at the house is a cat lounging in the windows of the house—a strange ghost since no cat currently lives here, nor is there a record of a cat ever living in the house. People report hearing a cat meowing, but after searching, can't find any feline. Where did this ghostly cat come from? Many believe it belonged to Benjamin Rush. A ghost cat haunted the Rush house. When the house was demolished, rather than haunt the garden as Rush does, the cat decided to move next door to more comfortable surroundings. Apparently cats are as mysterious after death as they are during life.

BENJAMIN RUSH HOUSE

One of the Founding Fathers, Benjamin Rush was a notable physician and neighbor to Bishop White. He signed the Declaration of Independence and became the first Surgeon General of the United States. He is also considered the "Father of American Psychiatry." When many fled the city during the yellow fever outbreaks, he stayed in his house once located on the corner of 3rd and Walnut Streets. And he might still be here, although his house was demolished. A colonial figure believed to be Dr. Rush has been seen walking through the eighteenth-century-style evergreen and holly garden.

Chapter 3
Revolutionary Buildings

Ghostly footsteps, foul odors, cold spots, and full-bodied apparitions are just a few of the things people have experienced around Independence Park. Timid park rangers assigned here don't last long, since they seem to be a favorite target of the ghosts.

CARPENTERS' HALL
320 Chestnut Street

James and Hazelle O'Conner had barely fallen asleep when the sound of someone walking on the floor above woke them up. Since they were supposed to be alone in the building, they thought someone had broken in. However, this burglar sucked at his job—his heavy footsteps echoed through the old building.

James picked up the phone and called the police. "I am the resident caretaker for Carpenters' Hall," he explained. "Someone has broken in and is walking around the attic."

The couple put on their robes and watched out the window for the two dispatched officers to arrive. Rather than leave their rooms and risk confronting the intruder, they opened their window and tossed the front door key down to the officer.

The two officers unlocked the door and climbed the stairway, past the second floor where the O'Conners waited nervously, to the attic where they had heard the noises. They searched the entire floor but found nothing but dust.

"But we both heard them," James insisted. "Someone was up there."

"Maybe it was a raccoon or possum," one of the officers said. "From the smell, at least one animal must have gotten in and died up there. It's really foul."

"It wasn't an animal. We heard footsteps," Hazelle said.

"Look, you're not the first caretaker to call us," the other officer explained. "I've been out here before on similar complaints but it is always the same. No one is up there. These old buildings settle at night, you know. Causes them to make all sorts of sounds."

The couple thanked the officers for coming out and James walked them out, locking the door behind them. But when he returned to the second floor, neither he nor Hazelle could relax enough to go back to bed. Knowing what they heard wasn't the sound of the building settling, they decided to investigate themselves. Slowly they ascended the stairs to the attic, but they stopped as soon as the horrible odor reached them. They tried to endure it enough to continue their search, but it was too strong. Retching, the couple retreated back to their apartment for the night.

The Carpenters' Company of the City and County of Philadelphia built Carpenters' Hall in 1770 as a headquarters and meeting house for the 200 members of the craft guild. It housed the First Continental Congress, which met for seven weeks in 1774. During the Revolutionary War, both sides used it as a hospital. In 1791, it was used as the First Bank of the United States.

Other organizations rented the building as well through the years, until 1856 when the Carpenters' Company renovated the building and restored it back to its original glory. After renovations, the Carpenters' Company employed resident caretakers for the building. The O'Conners were hired in this capacity in 1960.

The following morning, the O'Conners returned to the attic to find the source of the smell. They had to get rid of whatever stank before the smell polluted the entire building. But to their surprise (and relief) the odor was gone. Not even a lingering whiff of a stench remained.

A few nights later, the footsteps returned. Hazelle glanced at the clock: 2:10 a.m. Not wanting to call the police and look like fools a second time, the couple waited it out. For twenty minutes, heavy footsteps clomped around. When it stopped, James threw on his robe and decided to investigate. But the smell hit him when he opened the door, and he changed his mind.

When it happened a third time, Hazelle wanted to leave. No job was worth being woken up in the middle of the night. James convinced her that they just needed to adapt. Every night, they turned on the TV in their living room before closing their bedroom door. The TV drowned out any other noises in the building and allowed the couple to get their sleep.

According to Elizabeth Hoffman's *In Search of Ghosts*, the third floor wasn't the only area of the building that caused the couple problems. The basement, where Hazelle did the laundry, also caused problems for the couple.

To get to the basement, Hazelle had to walk down a narrow, winding staircase—a difficult task made even harder when she had to carry a load of laundry. So Hazelle brought a chair down where she could wait for the laundry to finish. The first day she did the laundry, nothing unusual happened.

The second time, as she passed by the chair, laundry basket in hand, the chair toppled over. Hazelle paused, righted the chair, and then set her basket on top of it. The chair fell over again, spilling her laundry all over the floor.

Hazelle rushed up the stairs, leaving the laundry behind. She called James at his office, but she couldn't reach him. As she waited for him to call her back, she thought about what she would say to him and realized how silly she would sound. She was frightened by a chair? Crazy! She couldn't tell him that. She decided to face her fears and headed back to the basement to finish the laundry.

This time, however, she took her dog with her. The dog might be small, but it would keep her company and keep her imagination from running away from her. She carried the dog downstairs, set him on the floor and reached down to pick up the laundry.

The dog immediately started growling. Hazelle had never seen the dog react like that. She looked around the room but couldn't see anything that would cause the dog's behavior. Before she could reassure the dog, he tucked his tail between his legs and dashed up the stairs as fast as his little legs could carry him. Hazelle decided he had the right idea and followed after him. The laundry could wait.

Hazelle wasn't the only one who felt that way about the basement. One weekend, their son was visiting. Since their living quarters were cramped, they made him a bed in the basement. But before long, he came back up, sleeping bag in hand, and announced he would crash in the living room. He couldn't explain why, but the basement made him uncomfortable, like something was watching him.

The hauntings at Carpenters' Hall appear to be connected to the nation's first bank robbery, which occurred at Carpenters' Hall the night of Saturday, August 31, 1798. The next morning, $162,821 was missing from the basement vaults that belonged to the Bank of Pennsylvania. That would be approximately $3 million today. Since there was no sign of forced entry into either the building or the vault, it had to be an inside job.

Suspicion immediately went to Pat Lyon, the man hired to change the locks on the vault. Lyon had left Philadelphia two days before the robbery, which should have cleared him, but this only convinced authorities of his guilt. However, when he learned he was the prime suspect, Lyon returned to Philadelphia to defend his good name. He was promptly locked up and spent three months in Walnut Street Jail. His bail had been set at $150,000. Ironically, the only way Lyon could pay such a sum would be to rob a bank. Since he hadn't, he had to stay in jail.

It wasn't until Isaac Davis began depositing the stolen money into Philadelphia banks (including the one from which he took the money) that the real culprit was caught. After a bank teller confronted Davis on December 19, 1798, he made a deal with the Governor of Pennsylvania. In exchange for returning the money and giving a full confession, Davis received a full pardon. He never spent a single day in prison.

However, Davis's confession wasn't enough to get Lyon released. Authorities were still convinced that he was involved. He managed to make bail on December 12, 1798, once it had been reduced to $2,000. But he still had to face a grand jury in January 1799, which did clear him of any wrongdoing. He later filed a civil suit against several bank officials and a constable and won enough money to live out the rest of his life comfortably.

Davis had been helped by bank porter Thomas Cunningham, who slept in Carpenters' Hall the night of the robbery. The Carpenters Company rented out rooms in the attic to single members of their guild, like Cunningham. Cunningham died in his room at Carpenters' Hall five days after the robbery, a victim of the yellow fever epidemic that was ravaging the city.

Shortly after his death the attic hauntings began. Heavy footsteps walking down the hallway to and from his room and on the stairs were reported as well as loud, unexplained noises from his room. The noises and foul odor continued even after the Carpenters stopped renting out rooms.

The reason Cunningham's ghost would produce a foul odor may have to do with how he died. The toxic phase of yellow fever affects several systems in the body. Bleeding from the mouth, nose, eyes, and stomach can occur with vomiting, none of which smells pleasant. The smell is likely his way of letting people know it's him.

The O'Conners also reported another strange event in 1974 when Philadelphia was celebrating the bicentennial of the first Continental Congress. The First Continental

Congress met in the building from September 5 until October 26, 1774, while Independence Hall was being used by the moderate Provincial Assembly of Pennsylvania. In celebration, Governor Milton Shapp decided to hold a meeting in Carpenters' Hall, which stirred the Congressional ghosts.

In the middle of the night the caretakers were woken by the sound of men talking, sometimes quite loudly, and what seemed to be the scraping of chairs on the first floor. Since they were used to odd noises in the building at night, they didn't investigate until the following morning. When they opened the doors to the meeting room, they found nothing had been disturbed, but could detect the smell of fresh tobacco smoke. Obviously Congress had decided to relive events from two hundred years earlier. (At least one Congress in the United States is still working.)

Since then, employees and visitors to Carpenters' Hall continue to report hearing noises coming from the meeting room or smelling tobacco in the room (although the entire building is nonsmoking).

INDEPENDENCE HALL
520 CHESTNUT STREET

In June 1994, a security guard was securing Independence Hall for the night. After locking the doors and setting the alarm, he did a final check of the building. While walking through the hall between the Declaration and Supreme Court Chambers, he saw a figure standing on the main stairs. As the guard approached him, he noticed that it was a man dressed in a Revolutionary War uniform. Since reenactors are common in Independence Park, the guard wasn't alarmed. Nope, not until the figure descended two stairs and vanished.

That same month, a Federal park ranger watched as a white smoke or mist filtered through the main door of the building. Before his horrified eyes, the smoke started to develop into the figure of a man dressed in a dark coat, light-colored britches, and a tricornered hat, just like clothing in colonial days. Before the specter could fully form, it vanished, as did the park ranger.

In a similar instance, a security guard on patrol heard footsteps on the second floor. He investigated but found nothing unusual other than a musty smell and an icy-cold draft at the top of the stairs. As he approached the gallery, he saw a white mist. Again it started to form the shape of a man and then vanished. (Maybe it needs some ghostly Viagra to prevent its premature evaporation.)

Independence Hall was completed in 1753 for use as a statehouse by Pennsylvania's colonial legislature. The red brick building consists of two small wings connected to a central building with a bell tower and steeple. The steeple was the first home of the Liberty Bell. The original steeple was removed in the 1780s, and the bell was lowered to the highest chamber of the brick tower. Then in the 1850s, the bell was moved to the ground floor where it remained on display until 1976, when it was moved across the street to the Liberty Bell Center.

The building became the principal meeting place for the Second Continental Congress from 1775 until 1783. The Founding Fathers met in the Assembly Room to sign the

Declaration of Independence in 1774. They met there again in 1787 to lay the framework for the Constitution. Also in this building, George Washington was nominated Commander in Chief of the Continental Army on June 15, 1775, and Benjamin Franklin was appointed the first Postmaster General.

The Georgian-style building is a symbol for the city of Philadelphia, although this style can be seen other places. A number of buildings were inspired by or replicate the design of Independence Hall. Most notable is the Hall of Presidents at Walt Disney World. Independence Hall itself has been seen in the movies *National Treasures* and *Shooter.*

Any building with this much history should have a couple of ghosts lingering, like the ghostly figures seen walking around the first floor or in the clock tower. Perhaps the scariest story occurred in 2002, according to Tim Reeser in *Ghost Stories of Philadelphia, PA.*

In the middle of the night, an alarm indicating that an intruder was in the building went off. Two park rangers were dispatched and searched the building from top to bottom. They didn't find anyone or anything. The men locked up and radioed to headquarters that everything was okay.

"No! Someone is in there," headquarters radioed back. "Go back in."

The two men complied and searched the building a second time. Again, nothing was found, a fact they quickly relayed back to headquarters.

"I'm looking at you on the monitor," said the ranger back at headquarters. "There's a man standing right next to you!"

The two men turned around, but the only two figures they saw were themselves. Terrified, the men raced out of the building. They transferred to other locations after that night.

So who is the misty ghost? Some say it might be Ben Franklin. After all, Franklin's ghost is notorious for haunting his favorite places. Others suggest it might be Benedict Arnold, although he has no real connection to the building the way Franklin does. But he might be looking for his wife. . . .

In the 1990s, a park ranger who worked at Independence Park repeatedly reported seeing a figure resembling Peggy Shippen, Arnold's wife, wandering around near the Hall. He believed that she was trying to return to Philadelphia, something she tried unsuccessfully to do during her life. When Shippen learned her husband was a traitor, she decided to leave him and return to Philadelphia. The city (as well as the state) refused to have anything to do with her. She was banished from both.

CONGRESS HALL
Chestnut and Sixth Streets

According to park rangers, the ghost of Marie Antoinette haunts the second floor of Congress Hall, located at the west end of Independence Hall. At least, that is what a newspaper article published in 1991 by the Associated Press said. No one knows how the story got started, but everyone agrees that it must have something to do with her portrait.

In 1784, King Louis XVI of France donated paintings of himself and his wife, Marie, to Congress. This sounds narcissistic of Louis, but Congress requested the portraits in a letter so "the representatives of these States may daily have before their eyes, the first royal friends and patrons of their cause." They also asked for more money to help them fight the "common enemy," aka England.

Ironically, these patrons of the Revolutionary War ended up being beheaded by their own people during the French Revolution just eight years later. When the capital was moved from Philadelphia to Washington, D.C., the paintings moved with it. Then in 1814, they disappeared and everyone assumed that the British burned them or they were stolen during the War of 1812. Whatever happened, they had not been seen since.

Then, in May 1976 French President Valery Giscard d'Estaing presented two portraits to Independence Park as replacements for the original ones. Maybe Marie decided to haunt Congress Hall since it is a place she is honored. Who can understand royals, especially royal ghosts?

Chapter 4

Historic
Buildings

*Alexander Hamilton served on George Washington's staff and is
considered one of the Founding Fathers, but it wasn't until after the
war that he founded the first bank and fought in a legendary duel
that ended his life and created his ghost. Conflict between two men
also created the ghosts at Merchants' Exchange, although that is
the only similarity between the two following stories.*

FIRST BANK OF THE UNITED STATES
116 SOUTH THIRD STREET

Alexander Hamilton championed a plan to establish a
national bank in order to expand the government's fiscal
and monetary power. Not everyone agreed. Two of Hamilton's biggest opponents were James Madison and Thomas
Jefferson, who called the banking industry "an infinity of
successive felonious larcenies."

Despite the opposition, the First Bank of the United
States was established in Philadelphia in 1791. It was first
located in Carpenters' Hall and then moved to a new building constructed specifically for its use in 1797. By that time,
Hamilton had resigned as Secretary of the Treasury after an
extramarital affair had become public.

After leaving his position, he returned to New York to
practice law, but he still had significant influence in politics.

During the 1800 election, Hamilton helped Thomas Jefferson defeat Aaron Burr when the Electoral College votes had the two tied for the presidency.

This event was one in a string of events between Burr and Hamilton. The two were political rivals and enemies. By 1804, Burr's political career was in a downward spiral. He needed a victory to improve his image, and he decided a victory on the dueling field would do. So he challenged Hamilton to a duel over comments Hamilton made at a dinner party several months earlier and demanded an apology for fifteen years of insults.

Hamilton was screwed. If he admitted to Burr's charges (which were true) or if he refused the duel, he would lose his honor—a bit ironic since in 1897 Hamilton admitted to having a three-year-long affair with a married woman and paying her husband $1,000 in blackmail money to prevent him from revealing the affair to his family. Hamilton had also been instrumental in passing a New York law that made it illegal to send or accept a challenge to a duel.

But making an action illegal didn't make it unpopular or prevent it from happening. Hamilton was honor-bound to accept the duel. The duel would be at Weehawken, New Jersey, the same spot where three years earlier, Hamilton's nineteen-year-old son, Phillip, died after his duel with George Eacker. Eacker had made a derogatory speech about Phillip's father.

Early in the morning on July 11, 1804, the two men faced each other with .56 caliber dueling pistols. Hamilton's shot went into a tree near Burr. Burr's shot went into Hamilton. Mortally wounded, Hamilton was taken across the Hudson to the home of a close friend, William Bayard. He died the following afternoon.

No one knows exactly what happened. The popular belief is that Hamilton, intent on missing, fired first. Burr, who fired second, deliberately struck and killed Hamilton. This sounds like Burr intended to kill Hamilton. However, Hamilton had not followed the standard procedure for intentionally missing—which was to shoot into the ground—so Burr had no way of knowing whether or not Hamilton had meant to hit him. Burr knew that if he missed his shot, Hamilton would have a second chance to shoot. Therefore, Burr likely took the shot in self-defense.

At the time, people didn't view it that way. Burr was indicted for murder and for the misdemeanor of "challenging to a duel," the law Hamilton had championed. He was also charged with murder in New Jersey. Burr fled to Washington, D.C., where he was immune from prosecution because he was the current Vice President of the United States. The murder charges were eventually dropped, but he was convicted of the misdemeanor dueling charge, which meant he could not vote, practice law, nor occupy a public office for twenty years.

After his death, Hamilton's ghost appeared frequently at the First Bank of the United States. Perhaps he wanted to relive one of the greatest achievements of his life. The sightings became so frequent and bothersome that Stephen Griard called in a priest to bless the building after he purchased it in 1811. The blessing decreased, but did not eliminate, the sightings of Hamilton at the bank.

The Burr-Hamilton duel created other hauntings. Alexander Hamilton also haunts Bayard's former home on 27 Jane Street in Greenwich Village, New York. People have reported hearing footsteps walking the halls and creaking on the stairs, doors opening and closing, and a toilet flushing at random. A man dressed in eighteenth-century clothes and resembling Hamilton has also been seen.

Alexander Hamilton has been seen around his tomb at Trinity Church, New York. People report seeing shadowy figures walking through the cemetery. Since the sightings increase around the time of the duel, many believe the ghosts of Burr and Hamilton are still feuding there.

Not to be left out, Burr also has three different places he is said to be haunting. The restaurant One if by Land, Two if by Sea, which was once Burr's carriage house, is haunted by Burr and his daughter Theodosia. He is an unhappy ghost. He has crashed dishes and moved chairs out from under patrons. Theodosia was traveling by ship from South Carolina to visit her father when it was besieged by pirates, who made her walk the plank. She made it home, if only in spirit, to the restaurant because it is the only remaining part of her New York home. Ladies beware: Theodosia likes to yank the earrings off women in the bar.

The Morris-Jumel Mansion at 65 Jumel Terrace, New York City, New York, was Washington's headquarters during the Revolutionary War and then home to Eliza and Stephen Jumel. Eliza and Burr were having an affair when Stephen was found dead. He "fell out of a window and onto a pitchfork"—or that's what she claimed. Eliza wasn't too upset; she quickly married her Burr. The couple divorced three years later. Burr died the day their divorce was finalized. Eliza died nearly three decades later, in 1865. All three (Stephen, Eliza, and Aaron) are believed to haunt the mansion. Eliza is often seen wandering the mansion in a white dress, although in 1965 she was seen by a group of schoolchildren who claimed she was riding a horse and wearing a purple dress.

Aaron Burr also haunts the Logan Inn in New Hope, Pennsylvania. He was a frequent visitor there and may have stayed there after the duel. Burr has to share the space with a number of other ghosts haunting the building, however.

SECOND BANK OF THE UNITED STATES
420 CHESTNUT STREET

In May 1905, Julia McGlone was leaving her job when she was attacked near the front of the building. According to McGlone, something jumped out of the shadows and grabbed her. The cleaning woman fought back, screaming and clawing at the attacker's face and neck. A nearby police officer ran to her rescue and attacked her assailant, but was thrown off him "like a rag doll." In response, the officer drew his gun, but the figure "blew flames out of his mouth" before leaping to the top of the steps and fleeing the scene. McGlone described the character as having claws and fiery eyes, and wearing a tight-fitting oil-skin outfit and helmet.

To many, her description of the attacker sounds similar to a devilish ghost known as "Spring-heeled Jack." Jack first appeared in London in 1837 when he attacked Mary Stevens in a similar way. He leaped out from an alley and grabbed her. He then ripped at her clothing and touched her with his claws. When Stevens began screaming, her attacker fled.

For the next sixty years, this unknown creature roamed the countryside of England. He was described as tall and wearing tight oil-skinned clothing and a helmet. Beyond that, he had claw-like hands, burning eyes, and was able to spit fire and jump long distances. He last appeared in Liverpool, England in 1904.

Did Jack travel from England to the States? Possibly. Or perhaps McGlone had read the stories about him and used those descriptions to elaborate her own story. Whatever happened, the 1905 attack remains the only reported sighting of Spring-heeled Jack in Philadelphia.

MERCHANTS' EXCHANGE
143 SOUTH THIRD STREET

Stand outside the Merchants' Exchange Building after the sun sets and you may see a man dressed in elegant 1830s attire standing on the portico. He stands there for a moment until the sound of hoofbeats echoing on cobblestone causes a panicked look to appear in the man's eyes, and he vanishes.

The ghost is that of Harold Thorn, a wealthy businessman in Philadelphia in the early 1800s. Thorn was mean, ill-tempered, greedy, and unscrupulous. If he hadn't been so rich, most people would have avoided doing business with him. But he couldn't be avoided when he came to the Merchants' Exchange Building to conduct business, as did many other businessmen in Philadelphia.

Jack Osteen was a "blind beggar" who often hung around outside the Exchange. Unlike Thorn, Jack had every reason to curse his life. His blindness made it difficult for him to find regular work, and so he often waited outside the building where the men tethered their horses, hoping someone would hire him. Despite his circumstance, Jack remained friendly and kind. While he waited for work, he sang or told stories. Jack also loved horses. He petted them and even gave them apples whenever he could.

One horse that bonded with Jack belonged to Harold Thorn. Given Thorn's nature, it is likely that Jack was the

Should Be Haunted:
Edgar Allan Poe House

532 North Seventh Street

Edgar Allan Poe first visited Philadelphia in 1829 and rented several houses in Philadelphia between 1837 and 1844. Only the house on Seventh Street survives. No one knows which of the thirty-one stories he published during this time was written here, but the basement described in *The Black Cat* eerily resembles the basement in this house.

Although Poe is famous for writing horror stories, they comprise only a small portion of his works; he is, however, credited with creating the genre of detective fiction. A statue of a raven perches out front of the house in honor of Poe's famous poem. The real raven that inspired Poe's poem can be found in the Rare Books department of the Philadelphia Free Library. Once the pet of Charles Dickens, it was preserved with arsenic and mounted on a log inside a shadow box.

only person who showed the horse any kindness. The horse grew so fond of Jack that he would refuse to be tied up unless he were put as close to Jack as possible.

The Merchants' Exchange Building was designed by William Strickland in the Greek Revival style on a triangular site bound by Dock, Third, and Walnut Streets. Built between 1832 and 1834, it was designed as a central meeting place for local merchants. Previously, merchants met in local coffee-houses. As the city grew, this practice became too difficult so merchants formed the Philadelphia Exchange Company and constructed the building as a central meeting place. The Exchange dissolved during the Civil War and the building was eventually purchased by the National Park Service.

November 12, 1834, was a lousy day for Thorn. He had come to the Merchants' Exchange hoping to increase his fortune, but he ended up losing a considerable amount of money. Thorn wasn't a good loser. The more he thought about his losses, the angrier he became. By the time he was outside, he was in a vile mood.

As he walked over to get his horse, he bumped into Jack. Jack tried to sidestep, but stepped on Thorn's expensive shoes. Thorn snapped. He raised his walking stick and struck Jack with a punishing blow, repeatedly. By the time someone managed to pull him off, Jack was dead.

For a moment, no one moved or said a word. Suddenly, Thorn's horse let out a colossal shriek, reared up, and smacked Thorn with his hooves. Thorn was mortally injured and died from his wounds. The event is known as Osteen's Revenge or Osteen's Poetic Justice. Since then, Thorn and the horse keep recreating the event. Every time Thorn appears, the horse arrives to chase him away.

Chapter 5

Never
Wed

Ghosts often have unresolved issues that keep them here on Earth. The Coleman sisters are two women who left this world before they could marry. Their spiritual sister of sorts can be found at the City Tavern, where a bride tragically died on her wedding day.

COLEMAN SISTERS
Intersection of Sixth and Chestnut Streets

Everyone should visit Philadelphia in July when the city gears up to celebrate Independence Day. Sure, lots of cities have fireworks, but Philly has the sites where the events actually took place. Maggie was one of several thousand visiting Independence Park recently. The sites were closed, but she was enjoying walking around as the city settled down from the day's festivities. As she approached Congress Hall, she observed two women dressed in eighteenth-century clothing.

The women walked arm-in-arm along the red-brick sidewalk past where Maggie was standing. Considering the number of historic reenactors she had seen, she didn't give the women a second thought. But then she decided they made a cute picture that she wanted to capture. She pulled out her phone and turned around to snap her shot, but the women had vanished. Later, back in her hotel, she told the story to the front desk clerk. That's when she learned about Ann and Sarah Coleman.

Ann and Sarah were the daughters of Robert Coleman, one of the richest men in Pennsylvania. The family lived in Lancaster, Pennsylvania. Margaret, the eldest daughter, married Judge Joseph Hemphill, a prominent Philadelphia congressman. The next oldest, Ann, was slender with long black hair and dark eyes. The combination of her family's wealth and status combined with beauty made her the catch of the county. But she fell in love with a young lawyer, James Buchanan.

The two became engaged, but in October and November of 1819, business affairs caused Buchanan to focus more on his legal affairs and less on his romantic life. By December, the engagement was broken off. The reasons behind the breakup remain unclear but have been the subject for plenty of speculation.

Several stories explaining the breakup have surfaced. Buchanan allegedly told *Harper's Weekly* in 1856 that he had returned home later than expected after arguing a case before the Supreme Court. While he was gone, Ann's mother wanted a more "fashionable husband" for her daughter, and so she intercepted letters the two wrote to one another, causing Ann to believe that Buchanan had delayed returning because he was involved with "city belles." By the time Buchanan returned, Ann was engaged to another man.

Most historians discount the *Harper's* article, however, because it contains a number of factual errors that Buchanan would be unlikely to make. For example, it says Ann's only living parent was her mother, but her father didn't die until years later.

Another story suggests that Ann became frustrated by her fiancée's preoccupation with work and began to suspect that he was only interested in her money. To make matters worse, on his way home, Buchanan stopped to visit William Jenkins to discuss a Supreme Court case. While there, Jenkins's sister-in-law, Grace P. Hubley, engaged Buchanan in a casual conversation. Hubley then sent Ann a note implying James stopped specifically to visit her. Apparently, Hubley wanted a husband and thought Buchanan would do. Angered and jealous, Ann wrote a note to Buchanan breaking off their engagement and then left for Philadelphia to visit her sister. She left Lancaster on Saturday, December 4. Four days later she was dead.

The most reliable record of what happened was recorded by Judge Thomas Kittera in his diary. He met Ann on the street at noon on December 8 and described her as being "in the vigour [sic] of health. . . . She had been engaged to be married, and some unpleasant misunderstanding occurring, the match was broken off. This circumstance was preying on her mind.

He went on to write, "In the afternoon she was laboring under a fit of hysterics; in the evening she was so little indisposed that her sister visited the theatre. After night, she was attacked with strong hysterical convulsions, which induced the family to send for physicians, who thought this would soon go off, which it did; but her pulse gradually weakened until midnight, when she died. Dr. Chapman, who spoke with Dr. Physick, says it is the first instance he ever knew of hysteria producing death."

Despite what Kittera wrote, the speculation at the time was Ann died from an overdose of laudanum. Chapman, who attended Ann, commonly prescribed the drug in cases of hysteria. Ann could have used the drug to commit suicide or accidentally taken an overdose.

How she died didn't matter to Ann's friends and family—they blamed James Buchanan for her death, an opinion that spread through the town of Lancaster. In a letter written by a Lancaster resident, Hannah Cohren, to her husband on December 14, 1819, "I believe that her friends now look upon him as her Murderer."

As a result, Buchanan was prevented from participating in or even attending Ann's funeral. Desperate, he sent a letter to Mr. Coleman pleading with him to let him attend. The letter read in part:

I have lost the only earthly object of my affections, without whom life now presents to me a dreary blank. My prospects are all cut off, and I feel that my happiness will be buried with her in the grave. It is now no time for explanation, but the time will come when you discover that she, as well as I, have been much abused. God forgive the authors of it. My feelings of resentment towards them, whoever they may be, are buried in the dust. I have now one request to make, and, for love of God and of your dear, departed daughter whom I loved infinitely more than any other human being could love, deny me not. Afford me the melancholy pleasure of seeing her body before its interment. I would not for the world be denied this request.

The letter was returned to him unopened.

James Buchanan never married and even kept Ann's letters with him until he died. In a fateful turn of events, he decided to run for Congress instead of focusing on building his law practice as he intended to do when he married. The change of plans led him to eventually become President of the United States.

Buchanan placed under seal materials that would explain what caused the young couple to quarrel. However, he left a note ordering the papers to be destroyed unexamined. Executors of his estate complied. If Hubley was involved in the breakup, she received a bit of karmic justice. Although engaged three times, she never married, and she died after her dress caught fire while passing over a grate on her way home.

Six years after Ann's death, her younger sister, Sarah Coleman, fell in love with a young priest at the Saint James Episcopal Church, William Muhlenberg. But like her sister, Sarah encountered obstacles and conflict that broke up the engagement. Muhlenburg started an evening service to serve some of the poorer classes in the region. Captain Robert Coleman and several other powerful vestrymen at the church felt bringing the lower class into the church tainted it and was undesirable. They attempted to stop the services, but their efforts were unsuccessful.

This caused conflict between Muhlenberg and Captain Coleman, which in turned caused problems in the romance. Coleman ordered Muhlenberg from his house and told him never to return. The outlook appeared bleak for the young couple, but they remained engaged. Then, a few weeks later, on August 14, 1825, Robert Coleman died. The death should have cleared the way for the young couple to marry. But somehow Coleman was able to reach out from his grave and prevent the union. In his will, he left Sarah $50,000, but it was to be kept in a trust and inaccessible to her husband after she married.

Although no evidence suggests that Muhlenberg was interested in her money, the engagement was broken off. Like her sister, Sarah went to visit her sister Margaret after her broken engagement. And like her sister, she died during her visit, also of an overdose of laudanum.

Muhlenberg never married but committed himself to the church. He founded and headed the Flushing Institute (now St. Paul's College) on Long Island. He also established the Church of Holy Communion in New York City, which became well-known for its community services such as employment agencies, educational classes, and medical services. In fact, the infirmary established by him at this church later expanded into St. Luke's Hospital, where Muhlenberg became superintendent and chaplain.

According to legend, a third Coleman sister (whose name is unknown) also committed suicide. She slit her throat when her father refused to allow her to marry the man of her choosing. Because her death was obviously intentional, she is buried in an unmarked plot, as is the tradition of the church when someone commits suicide. Because Ann and Sarah's deaths were not considered suicides, they were buried in marked plots at the Saint James Episcopal Church Cemetery in Lancaster County.

As to why the sisters haunt Chestnut Street, Margaret and her husband lived at 144 Chestnut Street near the intersection of Sixth Street during the time Ann died. However, they moved to Strawberry Mansion in 1821, and Sarah likely died there.

The two tragedies created more ghosts than those seen in Philadelphia. The ghosts of James and Ann have been seen in the graveyard surrounding the St. James church, where Ann is buried. Sarah and her beloved have also been seen together on the streets of Lancaster.

Ann also haunts her former home, now a bed and breakfast called Inn 422. Ann's ghost has been known to blow out candles and open doors and windows. She has even remade beds, rearranged beds, and cleaned up. (Don't we all wish we had that ghost in our house?)

CITY TAVERN
138 South Second Street

In the mid-1970s, chef Walter Staib was getting City Tavern in shape. He had recently signed a contract with the government to take over the establishment, and planned to make it an interpretive experience and as historically correct as possible while still allowing modern touches, such as the use of credit cards.

One morning Staib arrived at the Tavern to discover all the place settings in the Cincinnati room had been changed around.

Was it a prank? He wondered. It didn't seem likely. The staff was still in training and he had been the last one to leave. He was positive he had locked the door behind him since it had still been locked when he arrived. City Tavern was part of Independence Park, making it a federally protected building. No one would possibly risk federal prison to move silverware around, right? Nope, the ghosts must have had fun and reset the tables.

City Tavern hosts not one but two ghosts. The first ghost is that of a waiter. No one knows who he is, but they know he was murdered and by whom. He died in January or February 1781. On February 4, 1781, Samuel Rowland Fisher, a prominent Quaker merchant, wrote about the murder in his journal. "This afternoon heard that one of the Waiters or Servants at the City Tavern had been run thro with a Sword and killed by an Officer. All those Officers now quartered in town had been invited by some of the Citizens to dine at the City Tavern & This Murder is said to have been done by One of them when drunk."

The next day he wrote, "Heard that the Waiter at the City Tavern was killed by a Man known by the Appellation of Colonel Craig. My distress of mind still continues without much intermission." Craig escaped prosecution for the murder, which may be why the waiter's ghost lingers at the tavern. Many visitors have reported seeing his bloody body falling to the ground on the spot where he lost his life.

The first City Tavern opened in 1773. Proximity to Constitutional Hall made it the unofficial meeting place for both the First and Second Continental Congresses. For sixty-one years, the tavern was a favorite spot in Philadelphia. Everyone from Benjamin Franklin to Thomas Jefferson had a drink there, and Paul Revere stopped there the night of his fateful ride. Thankfully, he was able to ride off after his stop, which is more than can be said for George Washington. Our first president had to sleep at the tavern the night of his inauguration because he was too drunk to ride to New York.

Sadly, in 1834 a fire destroyed the original structure where Washington and Franklin drank. The fire decimated the building and took the life of a young woman.

On Saturday, March 22, 1834, a young woman was preparing for her wedding, which was set to occur in the tavern later that day. While she and her attendants primped on the second floor, the nervous groom and his buddies joked around downstairs. No one had any clue of the misfortune about to ruin what should have been the happiest day of the couple's lives.

What happened next is unclear. Someone could have placed a candle too close to the curtains or knocked one over. The curtains and rug caught fire first, and then the flames spread to the bride's train. She was engulfed immediately. Her friends and family tried to put out the flames, but were unsuccessful. By the time they realized their efforts were futile, the room—including the only exit—was ablaze.

Hearing the panicked screams, the groom and his groomsmen tried to rescue them. But the flames spread too fast and they had no choice but to retreat. The fire consumed most of the building and killed the young woman. The building remained a charred shell until the city demolished it in 1854.

Then in 1948, Congress decided to create Independence National Historic Park, which included restoring the area around Independence Hall and some of the original structures, including City Tavern. Great care was put into making City Tavern a perfect reflection of the former building.

The bride who perished in the blaze is the most famous ghost that resides there. She has been seen quite often, dressed in her bridal gown, on the second floor and in the halls of the building, especially if a wedding is occurring. She is even gracious enough to appear in photos, often appearing as a ghostly mist in pictures featuring young couples. Her presence is often seen in the Long Room by tavern guests. Passersby on the street have also reported seeing a young woman standing in the window when no one is supposed to be in the building. The almost-bride is also believed to have caused one of the windows to crack, but she is otherwise harmless.

It is unclear if the waiter or the bride likes to reset the tables. Perhaps Staib should simply leave the silverware out and let the ghost do the work for him. . . . The chef also says that they must be on alert during functions because the ghosts like to turn off the air conditioning or heat.

On October 17, 2014, another fire occurred at City Tavern. The fire started in a dumpster next to the building. The tavern had to close for a couple of days, but damage was minor and no lives were lost. Was some spiritual intervention at play to prevent a second misfortune? Only the ghosts know for sure.

Chapter 6

Around Old
City

Not all the ghosts in Philadelphia's historic buildings found in Old City are connected with the Revolutionary War, although a revolutionary ghost has been seen at The Bourse. The pirate ghosts seen on Water Street are far older, however.

THE BOURSE
111 South Independence Mall East

In 1716, Richard Sparks's will designated the southeast corner of Fifth and Market Streets in Philadelphia for Seventh-Day Baptists forever. He died soon after writing this will and became the first person buried there. His wife was also buried there a few years later. The next recorded burial occurred in 1772, but other people were likely buried there in the interim. In the 1780s, ownership of the burial ground became murky, with two different congregations claiming it.

Then, in 1810 the Harmony Fire Company erected a building for their use on an unused portion of the land. This revived the ownership dispute by adding new blood to the multitude of claims. Then in 1822, Stephen Girard bought the property south of the Sparks Burial Ground. He then tried to have the Harmony Fire Company evicted from the neighboring property. In response, the Harmony Fire Company constructed a board fence against Girard's house and claimed they now owned it. Girard responded by moving the fence on the north side of the Sparks property, blocking the engine house's entrance.

Finally, the mayor stepped in and arranged a compromise: If the fire company moved by a certain date, it would get $400 plus any moving expenses. The minute the fire company left, Girard demolished their building and built a brick fence around the used portion of the burial ground. (Emphasis on the word *wall*, as no gate provided access to the area.) He then erected a marble slab on the west wall of the enclosure in memory of Richard Sparks and the few known burials on the site. In 1830, the two churches claiming ownership reached a settlement, which should have resolved the matter once and for all.

Girard passed away in 1831 and bequeathed the property to the city. Harmony Fire Company quickly revived their claim to the land, possibly with the support of one of the churches that once claimed ownership. They didn't win, but in 1838 the city did agree to reserve a twenty-five-foot by twenty-seven-foot piece of land for the burial ground. The deal included putting a gate in the wall on Fifth Street to provide access. In return, the Seventh Day Baptists had to keep the property in good condition.

This agreement held in 1859 when the Eastern Market Company built on adjoining land and was required to build around the graves. Then, in 1891, plans to build a commodities exchange put the Sparks Burial Ground in jeopardy once again. The graveyard had been neglected and was overrun with weeds and trash. At first, the plan was to allow the widening of Fifth Street to pave over the graves, according to a March 6, 1893, article in the Philadelphia *Times*.

The plan changed, though, and any remains that could be found in the cemetery were to be moved to the Cemetery of Seventh Day Baptists at Shiloh, New Jersey. At least, that is what Charles Keith said in his 1917 book, *Chronicles of Pennsylvania*. Philadelphia has a history of being rather blasé about moving cemeteries. Some of the bodies buried there may still be there.

The Philadelphia Bourse Building, the first commodities exchange in the United States, was completed in 1895 and Sparks Burial Ground had disappeared. In 1979, the Kaiserman Company purchased the building, renamed it "The Bourse," and renovated it. Renovations took three years and disturbed some of its former tenants.

A retired electrical union worker, Carl,* told Tim Reeser in 2004 about an encounter his coworker, Paul,* had in the building. The two arrived at the building early one winter morning and then separated to begin their individual projects. A short time later, Paul approached "with a look of fear on his face." Carl asked him what was wrong. Paul claimed he had seen two men dressed in Revolutionary War uniforms. He described them as "kind of fuzzy" and "just standing there staring at him." The experience frightened Paul so much that he left the building and refused to return.

Today, the Bourse is a commercial complex that houses both a retail and office complex. It also advertises the chance to "Meet Franklin's ghost." Don't get too excited. This is actually an interactive education experience with a Franklin look-alike. The real ghost of Ben Franklin is far too busy elsewhere in the city to appear here.

*Not their real names.

WATER STREET
Corner of North Water and Race Streets

If you ever stroll along Water Street, watch out for pirates! A ghost dressed like a pirate walks along Water Street. Some say one pirate haunts the street; others claim several pirate ghosts haunt here.

Water Street started out as a footpath in the 1700s. As more business built along it, it was called King Street. The name changed during the Revolution. (What? You thought "Freedom Fries" was an original idea?) Water Street ran through the middle of what Philadelphians called "Helltown." Helltown was north of Arch Street between Third Street and the Delaware River and was notorious for having a higher-than normal density of taverns.

In 1744, a Philadelphia grand jury consider it a "temptation to entertain apprentices, servants and even Negros" and the taverns as "little better than Nurseries of Vice and Debauchery." But despite this, they did nothing to change the atmosphere.

Although the Caribbean (and Pittsburgh) are more famous for pirates, Philadelphia had its share of run-ins with them. In the late 1600s, when William Markum was acting Governor of Philadelphia, the city was renowned for being "pirate friendly." Markum even allowed one of his daughters to marry a pirate, James Brown, who had sailed with Henry Every (Avery). Between 1715 and 1725, referred to as the last great piracy outbreak, the mouth of the Delaware River and Philadelphia was a frequent target for pirates.

Pirates convicted in Philadelphia in the 1700s were sentenced to death by hanging. Their bodies were then tarred and hung in a gibbet—a human-shaped iron cage—as a warning to other pirates. One convicted pirate, Thomas Wilkinson, had been sentenced to be hung on Windmill Island in the Delaware River and then hung on Mud Island (now Fort Mifflin) in gibbets. His gibbet was constructed, but several important and influential Philadelphians signed a petition asking for mercy and he was released.

So the Water Street ghost is not likely that of Wilkinson, but it could have been one of the other pirates executed in Philadelphia and now wandering the street where he once found pleasure. Most of Water Street was destroyed in the 1960s and 1970s when Interstate 95 was constructed. A small portion—the portion that was part of Helltown—remains north and south of I-676 between 95 and the waterfront.

INDEPENDENCE PARK BEST WESTERN HOTEL
235 CHESTNUT STREET

Working at a busy urban hotel, Jenn Hay was used to handling customer complaints. Customers complained the room was too cold or the bed was too hard. If she put a guest close to the elevators, he would complain about the noise. If she put them further away, the walk was too long.

Noise complaints were common. When they remodeled the building in the 1950s, they didn't insulate enough to soundproof the rooms. Loud TVs and people talking in the hall she could deal with. She hated the calls complaining about the children.

"Would you send someone to my floor please?" guests asked. "Children are running through the halls giggling."

But when they would investigate, they never found any children. Sometimes complaints occurred when children weren't staying in the hotel. She couldn't explain that one. She had no explanation for the guest who called in the middle of the night to complain that her bed was shaking.

Hay didn't know what the guest expected her to do. The hotel didn't have the old-fashioned beds that would vibrate if you put a quarter in them. They were normal beds. The only way the beds would shake was if the guests bounced up and down on them or the entire building shook.

Still, the guest sounded upset, so Hay sent one of the housekeepers, Carmen Colon, to go the room and determine what could be causing the bed to shake.

"Nothing there," Colon told her when she returned.

Figuring the woman had a bad dream, Hay didn't give the incident another thought and finished her shift. But the next night, the woman showed up at the front desk.

"The bed is shaking again," the woman said.

"Ma'am, as I explained last night . . ."

"Listen to me. I was sound asleep and the bed started shaking. Then I heard this voice saying, 'Get out! Get out! Get out the window!'" The guest took a deep breath to steady herself, but Hay could see her hands were shaking. "Then, as soon as it stopped, the phone started ringing. But when I picked it up *there was no one there!*"

"There was definitely something in that lobby," Jenn Hay told Steve Volk in a 2006 interview for *Philadelphia Weekly*. "There was a chandelier over the steps leading toward the atrium that would swing back and forth on its own." Hay also said she constantly felt like she was being watched whenever she worked at the hotel and would see shadows

Should Be Haunted:
Bellevue-Stratford Hotel

200 South Broad Street

The Bellevue-Stratford opened in 1904 as the "grand dame of Broad Street." The 1936 and 1948 Republican Conventions were held here as was the 1948 Democratic Convention. According to the hotel's website, every president since Theodore Roosevelt has stayed at the hotel, along with a number of other famous people, including Bob Hope, John Wayne, and Katherine Hepburn. Bram Stoker even worked on his book *Dracula* while staying here.

It's not the hotel's darker history that adds it to this list but an event that occurred in 1976 when Philadelphia was celebrating its bicentennial. From July 21 through July 24, 1976, the American Legion held its fifty-eighth state convention at the hotel. The location and time was chosen to celebrate the Declaration of Independence's 200th anniversary. Thousands of members of the American Legion attended the convention.

Three days later, on July 27, one of the attendees died from what appeared to be a heart attack. On July 30, four more people who attended the convention were dead. On August 1st, another six died. All who died complained of tiredness, chest pain, fever, and lung congestion. They also had all attended the convention in Philadelphia. Within the week, 221 people were in the hospital and thirty-four had died, most of them Legionnaires who had attended the convention.

Speculation over what caused the illnesses and deaths included everything from influenza to poisoning. The notoriety caused the hotel to close and be put up for sale.

It wasn't until months later that scientists determined the cause. It was the first verified outbreak of what is now known as Legionnaires' disease, after the first known victims. Legionella bacterium, which causes the disease, was found inside the HVAC system of the hotel. Health officials hadn't paid attention in 1974 when nineteen members of the Independent Order of Odd Fellows contracted the (then unknown) disease after staying at the hotel. Three of them died.

With thirty-seven deaths linked to the hotel, you would think that at least one would return to haunt it. Nope. Not one has been mentioned.

darting by, but always out of the corner of her eye. When she turned to look, she found nothing there.

Skeptics could mention that the hotel publicly acknowledged the hauntings at the same time they announced a paranormal seminar at the hotel. Randy Howat, vice president of the hotel's management company, quickly pointed out that the hotel "probably already has one of the lowest-vacancy rates in Philadelphia" and didn't need to advertise its ghosts to attract guests.

The building was constructed in 1856 for Elliot's Doll Manufacture and later a dry goods store. It housed a couple of other businesses before becoming the Independent Park Hotel in the 1950s.

SIDE HAUNTS: SHIPPEN WAY INN
418 BAINBRIDGE STREET

Guests and a former innkeeper reported hearing disembodied footsteps in the dormer room at the Shippen Way Inn. According to a former innkeeper, the former owner's daughter-in-law committed suicide in that room. On the outside, the bed and breakfast looks like what would happen if you hired two architects to build your bed and breakfast and they disagreed. Actually, the seven-room inn was created by joining two separate townhomes, both of which were part of the Oak Street houses built in the 1750s.

In 2003, the current innkeeper told Tim Reeser that he purchased the property from "Bow Wow Bowers." Bowers told him he lived in the townhome at 416 Bainbridge Street but purchased the property at 418 for his son as a wedding gift. Bowers also claimed he had escaped from Eastern State Penitentiary and shot a woman outside the property.

A Horace P. "Bow Wow" Bowers did live on the 400 block of Bainbridge in July 1987 when he shot a woman in front of his home. He was involved in the April 3, 1945, escape from Eastern State Penitentiary. Bowers was paroled in 1963 but went back to prison after being convicted of the 1987 shooting. He later died in prison.

Although there is no evidence of a suicide occurring at the residence, the former owner claimed the property had no plumbing or any other modern conveniences when he gave it to his son. This, combined with living next door to your in-laws, would be enough to send any woman over the edge. Shippen Way Inn has since closed and was listed for sale in 2012. As of 2015, the property had not been sold.

SIDE HAUNTS: CORNERSTONE BED AND BREAKFAST
3300 BARING STREET

Surprisingly, the only other "haunted hotel" in Philadelphia is the Cornerstone Bed and Breakfast, located inside a restored Victorian mansion built in 1865, a mere ten blocks from Eastern State Penitentiary. Many visiting ghost hunters who have stayed here have claimed that an "ethereal presence" of a female spirit haunts the house. When she is around, people report smelling a floral perfume, followed by someone tapping on their forehead.

Part Two
CENTER CITY

In Philadelphia, you don't go "downtown," you go to "Center City." That's the term locals use to describe the part of Philadelphia that existed before the Act of Consolidation in 1854. The Act expanded the boundaries of the city of Philadelphia and made them the same as Philadelphia County. Eventually, the city and county governments were merged into one, which is why Philadelphia County has no government structure.

Unofficially, Center City is the area between the Delaware and Schuylkill Rivers south of Spring Garden Street and north of South Street. It is also the part of the city originally laid out by William Penn. Both Old City and Independence National Historic Park lie within Center City, although they each have enough ghosts to have their own section. Other neighborhoods that lie within Center City boundaries include Chinatown, Washington Square West, Market East, French Quarter, Rittenhouse Square, and the more recently designated Gayborhood.

Chapter 7

Center City
Squares

William Penn designed Philadelphia with five open space parks or squares in the city. They were originally called North East Publick, Northwest, Southeast, Southwest, and Center (Centre) Square. All but Center Square were given new, more patriotic names in the early 1800s and are now known as Franklin, Logan, Washington, and Rittenhouse, respectively. And all but Rittenhouse Square are believed to be haunted.

Why isn't Rittenhouse Square haunted? This square doesn't have the notorious history of its brethren. It was used as a pasture for livestock. But when wealthy residents moved in around it, it became a park. It was never used for executions or burials like the others were.

CENTER SQUARE: PHILADELPHIA CITY HALL
1401 John F. Kennedy Boulevard

William Penn is a significant figure in Philadelphia, someone that residents learned the hard way doesn't like to be upstaged. Upstage him and you'll face his wrath.

William Penn is honored as the founder of Pennsylvania and well-known for planning and directing the design of Philadelphia. Because of this, Pennsylvania has built several statues in honor of Penn. The most famous statue is the thirty-seven-foot-high statue perched atop Philadelphia's

City Hall. When construction was finished in 1901, the figure, which peaked at 548 feet, rose above everything else and gave Penn a view of his beloved Philadelphia for eternity.

Or until the 1980s, when city planners relented to the pressure and allowed One Liberty Place to build higher than the statue. At the time, they had no idea of the effect their decision would have on Philadelphia or their beloved sports teams.

Before 1987, Philadelphia sports teams were successful. The Phillies won the 1980 World Series and the 1983 National League Pennant. The Flyers won back-to-back Stanley Cups in 1974 and 1975, and appeared in the finals four times between 1976 and 1987. The Eagles returned to the Super Bowl in 1980, and the 76ers reached the NBA Finals four times between 1977 and 1982, taking the championship in 1983. Two months after One Liberty Place opened in 1987, the "Curse of Billy Penn" began making itself known. It started when the Flyers lost the Stanley Cup Finals. They didn't make it back until 1997, when they lost again. The Phillies lost the 1993 World Series and the 76ers lost the 2001 NBA Finals. But the worst was the Eagles. They lost three straight NFC Championship games between 2001 and 2003. The only other team in NFL history to lose back-to-back conference titles is the Dallas Cowboys. In 2004, the Eagles finally made it to the Super Bowl (for the first time since 1980) only to lose to the New England Patriots by three points.

That wasn't enough to satisfy Penn. His curse is also blamed for Smarty Jones losing his bid for the Triple Crown in 2004. The thoroughbred's home was located just outside Philadelphia in Bensalem. Philly fans were also affected, either directly or indirectly, by the curse. During this time, they got a reputation for being rude and displaying unsportsmanlike behavior. (Although who could blame them when their teams kept losing?)

Then in 2007, ironworkers John Joyce and Dan Ginion attached a twelve-inch figurine of William Penn to the final beam of the newly erected (and newly tallest) Comcast Center, located at Seventeenth Street and John F. Kennedy Boulevard.

Although the original statue was stolen (perhaps by a Giants fan?), a second, slightly smaller one replaced it. Being the tallest point in Philadelphia once again seems to have pacified Billy. On October 29, 2008, the Philadelphia Phillies won the 2008 World Series. Coincidence? That's up to you to decide.

But, unfortunately for the Philadelphia Eagles, appeasing Penn's spirit is not enough to break their losing streak. They also have to deal with a much older curse that Vince Lombardi supposedly put on them.

In 1960, the Eagles defeated the Green Bay Packers and won the NFL Championship. It was the only loss that year for the Packers and their coach, the legendary Vince Lombardi. It was also the only time Lombardi ever experienced a playoff defeat. Lombardi swore it would "never happen again." Everyone assumed he was referring to the loss since the Packers went on to win five NFL Championships plus the first two Super Bowls under Lombardi's leadership as either coach or general manager.

But it seems Lombardi also meant that the Eagles would never win another National Championship game or take home the Super Bowl trophy. (You know—the trophy that was renamed the "Vince Lombardi Trophy" in 1970 in honor of the Packers' victories at the first two Super Bowls.)

The Eagles made it back to the National Championships on two occasions, in 1980 and in 2004. They lost both times. No one knows what will appease Lombardi's spirit and enable the Philadelphia Eagles to win again, but somehow I don't think his spirit will be appeased with a statue on the top of the Comcast Building.

City Hall's courtyard is rumored to be haunted as well. People report seeing a dark shadow at eye level. When they make a close examination, it appears to be feet swaying. Many believe it is the ghost of Joseph Hightower, who was executed here.

Hightower was a Native American who was accused of killing a Quaker family named Samuelson. He was convicted and sentenced to death in 1783. As he was taken to the gallows, he proclaimed his innocence and vowed to get his revenge from beyond the grave. A short time later, James Mann, the police officer who arrested him, drowned. Then the prosecuting attorney, Robert Tanner, died after he was run over by a carriage, which severed his windpipe.

That two major players in the trial died of suffocation was enough of a sign to most people that Hightower had done as he had promised. While this tale sounds convincing, no documentation of Hightower, Mann, Tanner, or the Samuelson family could be found to lend any credibility to this story. But just because it may not be Hightower's ghost, doesn't mean it couldn't be the ghost of one of the other men hanged here.

WASHINGTON SQUARE
WALNUT AND 6TH STREETS

Of the five blocks earmarked to be public squares, Washington Square is the only one that William Penn wanted to become a burial ground. In a 1704 letter to the mayor of Philadelphia, he said it should be "a common burying-place for the service of the city of Philadelphia for interring the bodies of all manner of deceased persons whatsoever."

The burial ground became popular because it was close to both the hospital and the Walnut Street Gaol. African Americans, poor people, suicide victims, prisoners of war, victims of small pox, and anyone not associated with a church were buried here in the 1700s.

But it wasn't just a potter's field. Several thousand Revolutionary War soldiers are also buried here. On April 13, 1777, future president John Adams described the grounds in a letter to his wife:

> I took a walk into the Potters Field, a burying ground between the new stone prison, and the hospital, and I never in my whole life was affected with so much melancholy. The graves of the soldiers, who have been buried, in this ground, from the hospital and bettering house, during the course of the last summer, fall and winter, dead of the small pox, and camp diseases, are enough to make the heart of stone to melt away.
>
> The sexton told me, that upwards of two thousand soldiers had been buried there, and by the

appearance, of the graves, and trenches, it is most probable to me, he speaks within bounds.

The place was also popular with doctors. Dr. William Shippen usually used the bodies of suicide victims and executed prisoners for his anatomical lectures. But if none were available, he would get a body from Washington Square. African Americans felt particularly targeted by the Shippen's body snatching and a group petitioned the city in 1782 to allow them to fence around "Potter's Square." Their petition was denied, and the citizens took it upon themselves to patrol.

One woman was particularly devoted to keeping bodies safe. John F. Watson recorded her efforts in his *Annals of Philadelphia*. Much of the book is filled with stories Watson collected from tales told to him by older citizens. As Watson states:

> Some of my cotemporaries [sic] will remember the simple-hearted innocent Leah, a half-crazed spectre-looking [sic] elderly maiden lady, tall and thin of the Society of Friends. Among her oddities, she sometimes used to pass the night, wrapped in a blanket, between the graves at this place, for the avowed purpose of frightening away the doctors!

The problem of body snatching eventually was resolved in 1795, when the City Council decided to close it—not by moving the thousands under the ground, but by planting trees and installing sidewalks.

And since the graveyard has not been moved, Leah continues her quest to protect it. Many people who see her mistake her for a homeless person, until they get closer. In the 1980s, a woman was walking her dog early in the morning when she saw a woman with a cloak kneeling on the pavement. The woman approached to see if everything was all right. But when she got close enough to see underneath the hood there was nothing there. As the woman recoiled in horror, the hooded figure vanished.

In 1994, a Philadelphia police detective reported seeing Leah early one November morning. He was making his way through Washington Square when he paused to pour his coffee into an insulated mug. That was when he noticed a hunched figure near Walnut Street. Like many, he thought she was a homeless person, but something about her bothered him. As he told Charles Adams for the book *Philadelphia Ghost Stories*, "I looked closely at her and the more I tried to get a make on her face, the more trouble I had seeing any face. Honest-to-God it was as if there was no face, no head, under the blanket that was wrapped over her shoulders!" Again, the figure vanished before the person's eyes.

The chances of seeing Leah increases whenever something occurs that disturbs the graves, something that happens enough that it doesn't even make the news. Construction workers are required to have an archaeologist on sight if the dig more than twelve inches beneath the ground, to record and preserve any artifacts. Although, some archaeologists are also doctors, and that may be why Leah is still upset—doctors are still getting ahold of the bodies buried there.

FRANKLIN SQUARE
200 North Sixth Street

Drive past Franklin Square Park around midnight and you might catch sight of a ghostly young woman. The woman strolls through the park, pausing occasionally to water the plants, before vanishing. The woman is believed to be the daughter or granddaughter of Edward Penington. Penington owned a house nearby on the corner of Race and Crown Street (now Lawrence Street). Lawrence Street no longer extends to Race, however.

But the ghost could be connected to Franklin Square Park. Originally called North East Publick Square, Franklin Square is one of the five original public squares set by William Penn's original plan for Philadelphia. In 1825, the name changed to honor Ben Franklin because local legend says he conducted his famous lightning-kite experiment here. Before it became a public park, the land was used as a cattle pasture, a horse and cattle market, a drill and parade ground during the War of 1812, and a burial ground. From 1741 to 1835, part of the square was used as a cemetery by the German Reform Church. Some bodies were moved and a plaque marks the graves that remain. The ghost could be a woman still buried underneath the park.

LOGAN SQUARE
200 NORTH NINETEENTH STREET

Although no specific sightings are associated with Logan Square, shadowy figures and a general feeling of unease are commonly reported around the Swann Fountain—not surprising, considering the history of the square.

William Penn's plan for Philadelphia included five squares, one of which was Logan's Square (although Penn called it Northwest Square). Locals also refer to it as Logan's Circle due to the large traffic circle created in the middle as part of the Benjamin Franklin Parkway. The ground was originally used as a potter's field and for public executions. The last public execution in Logan Square was of William Gross on February 7, 1823. In 1825, the city decided to create a park and renamed it Logan Square. The transformation did not include moving the graves.

In 1890, excavations for a drain pipe near 248 North Nineteenth Street uncovered an intact coffin. A hundred and ten years later, archaeologists identified sixty intact burials in Sister Cities Park, located in Logan Square across from the Basilica of Saints Peter and Paul. They decided not to exhume the graves.

Chapter 8
Society Hill

Society Hill is a neighborhood inside Center City loosely defined as the area between Walnut and Lombard Streets and Front and 8th Street. It was named after the eighteenth century Free Society of Traders. Today, the neighborhood has the highest concentration of original eighteenth- and nineteenth-century architecture than anywhere else in the United States. With such a connection to the past, no wonder a few former residents from that era have had a hard time leaving.

HILL-PHYSICK-KEITH HOUSE
321 SOUTH FOURTH STREET

In 2003, three employees were working on the third floor of the Hill-Physick-Keith House, better known as the Physick House, when a breeze scattered papers onto the floor.

"We'd better close the fireplace flue," one of them suggested as she knelt to gather the papers. "That's quite a draft."

"Impossible," her coworker assured her. "The flue was sealed years ago."

"But if it didn't come from the fireplace, then where—?" She looked up and noticed a shadowy figure standing in the hallway near the doorway.

Before they could react, the figure moved down the hall-way and disappeared into the wall. They had just met the gray lady of Physick House.

The house gets its hyphenated name from its three most prominent owners. Wine importer Henry Hill built the house in 1786. In 1815, Abigail Physick purchased the house and deeded it to her brother Philip. He expanded the house and lived in it until his death in 1837. The house was then passed on or sold to various relations, until "Elsie" Keith bought it in 1895. Elsie was Philip Physick's great-great-granddaughter.

Born in Philadelphia in 1768, Philip Syng Physick earned his medical degree from the University of Edinburgh before returning to Philadelphia to set up a medical practice with the help of his friend Benjamin Rush. He was one of the few doctors that stayed in the city to treat the ill during the 1793 yellow fever epidemic. He served as surgeon at Pennsylvania Hospital from 1794 to 1816, and then at Phila-delphia Almshouse from 1801 to 1816, and was a consult-ing surgeon to the Pennsylvania Institution for the Blind in 1821.

He was elected to first professor of surgery at the Uni-versity of Pennsylvania Medical School in 1805. He resigned to take the positon as the University's Chair of Anatomy in 1819, a position he held until he retired in 1831. During this time, he regularly lectured on surgery at Pennsylvania Hos-pital. For these many achievements, he has become known as the "Father of American Surgery."

On several occasions, people have seen the figure of a woman wearing a long flowing gown appear unexpectedly in the house. The ghost pauses occasionally, as if looking for something, before disappearing. Others report seeing a woman's face in the mirror. On another occasion, the son of a tour guide reported talking to a lady who vanished through the window. Many people believe the ghost in the house is Philip's ex-wife, Elizabeth Emlen.

Philip and Elizabeth married on September 18, 1800. They had seven children, three of which died in infancy. In 1815, the couple decided to separate and later divorced. The divorce papers do not say why they split, but several theories exist.

According to the legends, to keep Elizabeth calm during the divorce, Dr. Physick dosed her with opium. This left her in a dazed state and caused her to wander the house and the backyard where she frequently sat under her favorite tree. She died in 1820, five years after the divorce was finalized. The cause of death is unknown, but some speculate it was caused by an overdose of opium.

All was fine until her favorite tree was chopped down. Since then, a figure of a woman wearing a lavender gown has been seen and even heard sobbing in the garden. In some of the stories, Dr. Physick ordered the tree cut down while Elizabeth was alive.

Another legend says Elizabeth was addicted to opium and unstable. Her husband, fearing for the safety of the children, barred her from entering the home. Unable to get inside, she wandered around the backyard and peered into the windows, upset that she was not allowed inside. For those reasons, she has returned after death to gain entry to the home.

In reality, Philip and his wife divorced in 1815, the same year Abigail gave the house to her brother. Philip and his children moved into the house. Elizabeth stayed in her father's house before moving into a new house on Pine Street, according to a letter written by her sister-in-law, Susan. The letter also said her aunt was moving into the residence to be her companion and she hoped that "the solitude that poor Betsey has thus reduced herself may give time and occasion for useful reflection and thus be a means of leading her back to a better way."

Since Elizabeth never lived in the house on Fourth Street, she would be an unlikely candidate to haunt it. A better candidate is Elsie Keith. She spent roughly forty years in the house and extensively remodeled the house because she had an extreme phobia of dust. She removed baseboards and replaced them with white glazed tiles so the floors could be mopped. She also removed all the moldings (which caught dust), and removed the inside shutters, along with a variety of other items, to keep the house dust-free. Perhaps what the ghost is looking for is dust.

Keith has reason to haunt the house. In the 1960s, publisher Walter Annenberg bought the house and restored it to the state it was in when Physick lived in it. In other words, he undid the dust-ridding renovations that Elsie had done. Annenberg then donated the house to the Philadelphia Society for the Preservation of Landmarks, which has made it into a museum.

Others say the ghost is one of the many cadavers that Physick unearthed from local cemeteries to use in his surgical lectures—although these ghosts would be more likely to haunt Pennsylvania Hospital where the lectures took place and where, rumor has it, their bodies were then reburied.

(No historical evidence supports this tale, however.) One final rumor is the ghost is that of a former resident when the site contained an infirmary for the ill and insane. This last rumor has the most truth to it. The Spruce Street Alms House occupied the entire block between Third and Fourth Streets, and Spruce and Pine Streets. Built in 1732, it remained in use until a large almshouse was built in 1767 down the street.

POWEL HOUSE
244 SOUTH THIRD STREET

Powel House was built in 1765. Samuel Powel purchased it four years later when the original owner, Charles Stedman, faced debtor's prison. Samuel Powel was the last mayor of Philadelphia before the Revolutionary War, and the first mayor of the city after it. Since he sided with the colonies, he earned the title "The Patriotic Mayor."

The Powels were well-known for their hospitality and for being one of the central cogs around which high society in Philadelphia revolved. They entertained George Washington, Ben Franklin, John Adams, and the Marquis de Lafayette, among many other famous Revolutionary figures. Powel was even a pallbearer at Benjamin Franklin's funeral.

Powel was one of many who died during the yellow fever epidemic in 1793. His widow sold the house to her nephew in 1798. For the next hundred years the property changed hands a number of times. In 1917, owner Wolf Klebansky sold portions of the interior to the Metropolitan Museum of Art and other individuals and then used the stripped building as a warehouse. By 1931, the house was slated for demolition, but the Society for the Preservation of Historic

Landmarks was created to save it. By World War II, the house had been restored to its original state.

The first tales of hauntings can be traced back to a 1965 article in the *Philadelphia Bulletin*. In the article, historian Edwin Coutant Moore recounted several meetings he and his wife had with spirits in the house.

The first encounter occurred when he was descending the staircase between the second and first floors. He watched two men in uniform walking toward him. According to Moore, "One wore a blue uniform. He looked up and smiled pleasantly. His teeth were very white. Suddenly he was gone." Moore felt that the soldier in blue looked a lot like the Marquis de Lafayette, who was a frequent visitor when the Powels owned the house.

Gilbert du Motier, the Marquis de Lafayette, was a wealthy young nobleman whose parents died while he was boy. He learned of the American cause as a teenager and was determined to travel to America. Although originally rebuffed on his arrival in 1777, his passion and willingness to serve for free soon won over colonials, including George Washington.

He was given the title of Major General in the Continental Army. He faced his first major combat duty at the Battle of Brandywine in September 1777, where he was wounded in the leg. After he recovered, he joined Washington and the two endured the hardships of Valley Forge. For the next few years, Lafayette provided military leadership while securing resources necessary to ensure victory.

Moore's wife also had an encounter with a ghost on the second floor. She was entering the drawing room around twilight when she noticed a woman sitting in a chair fanning herself. The woman had black hair which was pulled up with pearls and wore a beige and lavender dress. Mrs. Moore said the spirit "turned and looked directly at [her]" but when she turned on the light, the chair was empty.

Several months later, Moore was looking for an authentic colonial dress to wear to a party they were throwing at the house. At a costume shop, she found a dress that looked exactly like the one worn by the woman she'd seen months earlier in the drawing room. The shopkeeper told her the dress was known as the "Peggy Shippen gown."

Peggy Shippen was the daughter of a prominent Philadelphia family and the wife of the notorious Revolutionary traitor, Benedict Arnold. It has been suggested that Peggy initiated the negotiations between her husband and her former lover, John André, resulting in Arnold's treasonous acts. André was an officer under General William Howe's command. André often visited both the Shippen and Powel homes, as well as the Chew House next door, during the British occupation of Philadelphia. (The Chews also owned Clivedon Manor.)

After André fled with the British forces in June 1778, Shippen met and married Benedict Arnold. The couple eventually resided in the Masters-Penn Mansion on Fifth and Market Streets, which happened to have been the home of General Howe during the British occupation. When Arnold's treason was discovered, he left Peggy and their newborn son behind. Afterwards, Peggy went to Philadelphia to stay with her family, but was banned from the city. She eventually joined her husband in England, only to discover that, although the British profited from their treason, they didn't approve of it.

For that reason, Peggy may have decided to return to Philadelphia where she was happiest. However, this doesn't explain why she has chosen to haunt a home to which she is not strongly connected instead of a home in which she once lived.

The Moores also described a ghostly visitor who kept a regular schedule. At 4:00 in the morning, the doors on the antique wardrobe in their upstairs bedroom opened on their own. When they decided to lock the doors to prevent the event, the bedroom door would creak loudly instead, as if the ghost was bothered that its routine was interrupted.

If the Moores were the only ones who reported ghostly activity, one could dismiss them as simply their attempts to create interest in the historic site. But other people have reported similar events.

In 1993, a woman named Cindy saw a woman on the second floor. "The first time I went into the Powel House, in the center hall at the top of the steps I saw a woman. I couldn't make out her face . . . but she was all in lace." She also described hearing ladies outside the drawing room. "I've heard them laughing, not laughing hysterically, but little chuckles and real quiet things like that."

Another man, Tom Donnely, also met a woman on the second floor. He was in the bathroom when the lights went out. As he tried to find his way to the stairs in the dark, he felt a "cold clammy grip" take his hand and lead him. As Donnely and the unseen guide made their way toward the stairs, the lights came back on. For just a brief moment, Donnely saw his guide standing next to him. She was a woman wearing a long dress and smiling—then her image faded away.

Benedict Arnold may also haunt the house. He has been seen throughout the house, specifically in the second-floor drawing room. Perhaps he has decided to join his wife or he is doing penance for his betrayal of the patriots.

REBECCA GRATZ CLUB
532 SPRUCE STREET

For several nights, a resident awoke in the middle of the night to find a beautiful woman standing above her. She was described as standing at the end of the bed, looking sad with her head bowed as if in mourning. Other residents and visitors to the four-story limestone and stucco apartment building just south of Washington Square report seeing the same figure who never says a word before she disappears before their eyes. Her identity is unknown, but she is believed to be a former resident of the Rebecca Gratz Club.

The "Club" was first used as a residence for poor, pregnant Jewish women and working girls. Then, in the 1950s, the building was converted to a nonsectarian halfway house for young women with emotional problems. Some say the ghost is Rebecca Gratz, a nineteenth-century Jewish philanthropist and the inspiration for Sir Walter Scott's Rebecca of York character in *Ivanhoe*. However, the building wasn't constructed until after she died.

Chapter 9
Holy Trinity of Ghosts

Churches don't always like to admit their churchyards are haunted—perhaps because the Old Testament says that anyone who consults the dead is "detestable to the Lord." But that doesn't seem to bother these three churches, remarkably located within a block of each other in Society Hill. These churches have accepted the ghosts that wander their churchyard cemeteries, perhaps because they date back to the Revolutionary War.

ST. PETER'S CHURCHYARD
313 PINE STREET

According to the St. Peter's Church website, "We are a congregation of young and old, married and single, gay and straight, people from all different backgrounds." That could pretty much describe their ghostly congregation, which meets rather frequently in the graveyard surrounding the church. Indian Chiefs, African Americans, and even a ghostly dog have been seen there.

Built in 1761, St. Peter's Church was the church of choice for Ben Franklin and George Washington. It remains just as it was in the eighteenth century, although the tower and steeple were added in 1842.

One of the most common ghostly sightings is that of a white figure in the church cemetery. But this job seems to be too immense for only one spirit, as several have taken on the role. One is a spirit that appears at 9:00 p.m. or 10:00 p.m. (Perhaps the ghost gets confused during daylight savings time.) Its gender is unknown but sightings of it date back to 1834. Most report that it walks stiffly through the tombstones in the same pattern each night, never acknowledging anyone or thing before it vanishes.

According to an article on Examiner.com by paranormal investigator Debe Branning, this ghost created a stir in October 1880 when its regular appearances drew a crowd. Sightings at this time suggested that it was the ghost of a child doing the hauntings.

The figure in white may be Stephen Decatur. Decatur was a naval officer who achieved many naval victories in the early nineteenth century. But he died fighting a more personal battle: the result of a duel with Commodore James Barron. He was forty-one years old. Decatur was placed in the tomb of Joel Barlow in Washington, D.C., and then moved to the church cemetery so he could be buried next to his parents. Perhaps it was his untimely death or moving his body that stirred his spirit.

Another white figure is a man walking his (also ghostly) dog. The figure protects the cemetery and has been known to chase away locals who bring their dogs too close to the cemetery. A female white figure with long hair and wearing a long gown has been seen by a former caretaker and members of a tour walking around the south section of the cemetery. She is also rumored to be protecting the cemetery, specifically the graves of several Indian chiefs.

In January 1793, a delegation of tribal chieftains arrived in Philadelphia for a peace council to resolve boundary disputes. According to parish books, chiefs La Gese, Apuatapea,

Bigigh Weautons, Barkskin, Grand Joseph, Toma, and Wape-teet died of yellow fever in January, and chief Little Elk died in April. No agreement was reached at the peace council. The Indians were defeated at the Battle of Fallen Timber in 1794. Although Washington buried them in the cemetery with full military honors, because they were not buried in a consecrated Indian burial ground, their spirits could not make peace. Their spirits were often reported moving restlessly through the cemetery. Supposedly, a ceremony was recently held here by their modern-day relatives so these spirits could find peace.

Finally, a phantom carriage has been seen and heard in and near the cemetery. Some report seeing the carriage being pulled by an invisible horse racing through the cemetery, knocking over tombstones and then disappearing as it approaches a wall of the church. Others report hearing the sound of hooves and wooden wheels on cobblestone near the church, but no ghostly sighting. One former caretaker reported hearing the sound and then seeing the ghost of an African-American man dressed in colonial clothing, suggesting that the ghost may be from one of the yellow fever outbreaks. (African Americans were believed to be immune to yellow fever and were enlisted to operate the carts that removed the dead from the city.) If that is the case, two different phantoms may haunt here.

According to John F. Watson in his *Annals of Philadelphia*, which was published in 1857 but written between 1830 and 1850, a ghostly carriage was seen in Philadelphia long before the yellow fever epidemics:

I have seen aged people who well remembered the town talk of the people about seeing a black coach driven about at midnight by an evil spirit, having therein one of our deceased rich citizens, who was deemed to have died with unkind feelings to one dependant (sic) upon him. I suppress names and circumstances; but there were people enough who were quite persuaded that they saw it! This was before the Revolution.

Perhaps the ghost has nothing to do with the church, and the church happened to be built on his route.

OLD PINE STREET CHURCH & CEMETERY
412 PINE STREET

Almost a block down Pine Street sits Old Pine Street Church where disembodied voices and other noises, cold spots, orbs, and Hessian soldiers are said to haunt its cemetery. Old Pine was established in 1768 by George Duffield. Duffield also served as the church's pastor and served as chaplain to the First Continental Congress in 1774. In fact, Duffield's speeches about independence were so powerful the British put a price on his head. When the British occupied Philadelphia on September 26, 1777, Duffield immediately sought out Washington at Valley Forge. He brought with him sixty parishioners to serve in the army.

While Duffield might have escaped the wrath of the Brits, Old Pine was not so lucky. The British used it as a hospital. The soldiers tore up the pulpit and pews to use as firewood. Once the church was stripped, they used it as a stable. Not even the cemetery was spared. The British first used it as target practice and then buried one hundred Hessian soldiers there. (Hessians were the "foreign Mercenaries" mentioned in the Declaration of Independence as helping the British complete "works of death, desolation and tyranny.")

But apparently the Hessians paid the ultimate price for what the British did to the church. Many believe that their souls are condemned to roam the graveyard as punishment. The Hessians did not remain buried there, however. They were moved to a mass grave somewhere outside the city gates.

The cemetery around the church dates back to 1764 (before the church itself), but graves from even earlier rest on the western side of the church. Those graves, which date from the early 1700s, were transferred from the First Presbyterian Church in 1850. Technically, the church is actually the Third, Scots and Mariners Church, since the Third Presbyterian merged with the Scots church in 1953 and the Mariners Church in 1959.

And if you get a sense of déjà vu when you visit, as if you've seen it before, it's not (necessarily) because you were a colonial in a past life. The church was seen in the 2004 movie *National Treasure*, starring Nicholas Cage. It is also the church passed by young Cole and his mother as they make their way to the funeral for the girl who was poisoned by her mother in *The Sixth Sense*.

OLD ST. MARY'S CHURCH & CEMETERY
252 SOUTH FOURTH STREET

North of Old Pine Street Church is St. Mary's Church and Cemetery, better known as Old St. Mary's. Although the church was built in 1763, its burial ground began in 1759 with graves moved from Old St. Joseph's and Washington Square's Catholic burial grounds.

St. Mary's Cemetery is not as notoriously haunted as the other churchyards, but it does have a couple of ghosts connected to one of its most famous interments: John Barry. John Barry was an officer in the Continental Navy during the American Revolutionary War and later in the United States Navy. He is credited as "The Father of the American Navy," a title he shares with John Paul Jones.

Two major tragedies befell Barry around the time of the Revolution. The first was the death of his beloved wife Mary Clary (Cleary) on February 9, 1774. She was only twenty-nine years old. Her death upset Barry deeply because he was at sea when she passed away. The second tragedy occurred four years later in August when the ship his brother Patrick was on disappeared at sea.

The ghostly female figure walking around the Barry tombstone is believed to be that of Mary. A male figure seen walking through the cemetery is believed to be that of Patrick. Although Patrick is not buried in the cemetery, his spirit may have found his way to say a final good-bye to his brother.

Chapter 10

Washington Square West

Washington Square West lies between Broad Street and Society Hill. M. Night Shyamalan once lived here, and the ghost stories about the Pennsylvania Hospital, Walnut Street Theatre, or Bonaparte House must have had an influence on him. After all, he wrote and directed The Sixth Sense, which was set and filmed in Philadelphia. Perhaps he was remembering some of the old ghosts from his neighborhood.

PENNSYLVANIA HOSPITAL
800 SPRUCE STREET

Benjamin Franklin and Dr. Thomas Bond founded Pennsylvania Hospital, the nation's first hospital, in 1751. A temporary hospital was established in a house until the hospital could be built on land purchased by the hospital at Eighth and Pine Streets. In 1767, Thomas and Richard Penn donated additional property, which gave the hospital the entire block. The hospital was created to care for "the sick, the injured and those suffering from mental and nervous diseases."

It wasn't long before the hospital achieved an excellent reputation. During the Revolutionary War, the hospital treated both British and American soldiers. After the war, Dr. Philip Syng Physick, the Father of American Surgery, and Dr. Benjamin Rush, the Father of American Psychiatry, both joined the staff. Rush's involvement with the hospital helped it gain a reputation for treating the mentally ill humanely, which led to an overcrowding problem after the Revolutionary War. One of the patients housed here was Mary Lum Girard.

Mary was the wife of Stephen Girard. According to the legends, Mary was nearly seventeen years old when she married the twenty-six-year-old Stephen on June 6, 1777. It was a regular Cinderella story: Mary was poor but very beautiful and Stephen was a wealthy suitor who asked for her hand in marriage.

But their marriage was no fairy tale. Mary had problems getting pregnant. Frustration over her infertility led them to seek comfort in the arms of other lovers. But what was good for the gander was not good for the goose.

In 1790, Stephen had Mary committed to the insanity ward of the hospital. Mary had a reputation for mood swings, sometimes violent ones if she was provoked, so her commitment wasn't a huge surprise. Three months after she was admitted, the hospital discovered she was pregnant and wanted to send her home. Pennsylvania Hospital didn't establish a maternity department (known as a "lying-in") until 1803. Before then, women gave birth at home.

Stephen insisted Mary stay at the hospital despite her pregnancy. He also denied the baby was his. People suspected that Stephen had Mary committed because she was pregnant with another man's baby. That way he could have her declared insane and divorce her.

His plan didn't work. At the time, the law did not allow insanity as grounds for divorce. He tried to push a bill through the Senate to change things, but it never passed.

Since he couldn't remarry, he kept several mistresses (usually referred to as his "housekeepers") including Sally Bickham, whose portrait hangs in Girard College's Founders Hall. No portrait of Mary Girard hangs at the college or anywhere else.

Mary gave birth to a baby girl four months later (seven months after her commitment). The baby was sent to a wet nurse after it was born and died five months later. Sadly, Mary spent the next twenty-five years locked away at Pennsylvania Hospital, not even escaping after death. It wasn't as bad as it could have been. Instead of being locked in the basement insanity ward, she was given a series of rooms that included a parlor on the hospital's first floor.

She died in 1825 and was buried in an unmarked grave on the grounds of the hospital (as was her baby girl). Today, exactly where she was buried has been lost. Her only marker is a plaque on the first floor of the hospital that mentions she is buried near that spot. Ironically, that same marker also honors her husband for his contributions to the hospital, which most say he did to keep her locked up there.

Perhaps this is why some say she still haunts the first floor and grounds of Pennsylvania Hospital. The ghostly figure of a woman has been seen by staff members, but when they approach her, she disappears.

WILLIAM PENN STATUE

On the lawn in front of the Pennsylvania Hospital sits another William Penn statue. William's grandson, John Penn, found it in an antique shop and donated it to the hospital in 1804. But its prominent position is not enough for the statue, which seems to feel overshadowed by its larger counterpart and has found a way to stand out on its own.

According to legend, the ghost of William Penn steps out of the statue at night and leisurely strolls through the gardens and halls of the hospital. Some say this event occurs every night at 6 o'clock. Others say that it only occurs during a full moon.

A rumor exists that the statue itself leaves its stand, but this has only been known to happen on one occasion. Back in June 1865 the statue fell off its pedestal after an unusually severe storm. The statue was reattached and since then it has stayed put—or rather it has made sure to return whenever it leaves.

BONAPARTE HOUSE
260 SOUTH NINTH STREET

The plaque on the front of a house on South Ninth Street reads "Joseph Bonaparte House 1813," but he doesn't haunt it. Joseph Bonaparte, deposed king of Naples and brother to Napoleon, rented the house from 1813 until 1816—a short time, but long enough to forever change the life of Chloris Ingleby.

Born on the wrong side of town, Chloris worked as a dancer but dreamed of being plucked out of poverty by a handsome prince. And she decided that prince would be Amadee la Fourcade, Bonaparte's steward.

Fourcade also dreamed of improving his circumstances, but that wouldn't happen if he married a dancer, especially an American one. He hoped to marry a Corsican girl related to the Bonapartes.

But Chloris refused to accept that Fourcade didn't love her and hatched a plan to keep them together. She would stow away on his ship, the *Jean Barth*, reveal herself once it

Should Be Haunted: Oregon Diner

302 West Oregon Avenue

On April 7, 1866, Anton Probst killed eight people: Christopher and Julia Dearling, four of their children, a young farm hand, and a woman visiting the Dearlings, Elizabeth Dolan. Probst was tried for the crimes and executed. After his body was dissected at a local medical college, his skeleton went on display in the college museum, where it remains today.

The location earned notoriety a second time in 1963 when Nicodemo Scarfo stabbed a longshoreman to death with a butter knife in a fight over a booth at the Oregon Diner. Scarfo was convicted of involuntary manslaughter and served a year in prison. The conviction didn't hurt his career; he eventually became the head of Philadelphia's organized crime.

had set sail, and convince her beloved to marry her. Shortly before Fourcade was scheduled to leave, she snuck onto the ship and hid in one of the holds.

Somehow, Fourcade learned of her plans. Rather than be flattered, he was irritated by Chloris's scheme. He put a guard outside the hold where she was hiding and waited. It took fifteen days before Chloris ran out of food and was forced to abandon her hiding spot.

The guards hauled the stowaway off the ship and took her to the Bonaparte House where Fourcade waited. Rather than showing her mercy or even pity, Fourcade snatched her by the hair and dragged her across the yard to the barn, where he tossed Chloris into one of the box stalls. He ordered her to be placed on a diet of bread and water. Fourcade then returned to France.

Already dangerously thin from hiding on the ship, the imprisonment would have killed Chloris, but her guards snuck her more nutritious food. After Fourcade left, one of the guards decided to help her and gave her a tool enabling her to saw through two of the bars of the box stall and escape.

For some unknown odd reason, instead of making a break for it, Chloris ran across the garden toward the rear of the house. She went up the porch stairs, leaving one of her slippers behind, toward the back door. The noise woke one of the guards, who immediately fired a shot. But by the time he lit a lantern, Chloris was nowhere to be found. Whether she escaped or died somewhere in the house remains a mystery. She was never seen again—at least not alive.

Her ghost is another story. Residents have seen the figure of a woman dressed in rags, sometimes with her hands tied behind her back, walking around the back garden and alley way next to the house. The sounds of sobbing and moaning are also heard here.

As for Fourcade, he returned to France only to find that the Corsican woman had married someone else. He was later shot and blinded in the 1830 revolution and was unable to travel when Bonaparte returned to Philadelphia in 1837. When Joseph Bonaparte learned what Fourcade had done, he said it was "dreadful of Fourcade" and that he was "a base traitor and a vile ingrate," according to a 1947 article printed in the *Altoona Tribune*.

SIDE HAUNTS: JOSEPH BONAPARTE

Although Bonaparte doesn't haunt the house on Ninth Street, he has been seen in nearby Bristol, Philadelphia. Joseph Bonaparte befriended a woman, Sarah Keene, who fell victim to her own romantic tragedy and became a recluse. She did, however, allow Joseph to visit her. Although her house is gone, her ghost has been seen in the Margaret Grundy Memorial Library, located at 680 Radcliffe St., in Bristol. Bonaparte, however, is seen near the riverbank carrying a lantern as well as floating along the Delaware River, as he often did when visiting Sarah.

Chapter 11
Off Broad
Hauntings

Broad Street is a major arterial street that runs for over twelve miles in Philadelphia. City Hall splits the street into two sections, north and south. These hauntings are located off South Broad Street in the neighborhoods of Washington Street Square West and Rittenhouse Square.

HISTORICAL SOCIETY OF PENNSYLVANIA
1300 LOCUST STREET

Dan Rolph, Historian and Head of Reference Services at the Historical Society of Pennsylvania, has gotten used to employees quitting. It's not because he's hard to work for or the job is unpleasant. Some people have trouble accepting disembodied voices, unexplained footsteps, elevators moving on their own, and shadowy forms that disappear in the building. But that's what happens when you work in a building haunted by several ghosts.

The Society was originally located in a house that belonged to General Robert Patterson, a general in both the Mexican-American and Civil wars. Between 1905 and 1909, the society demolished the house and built the current building.

Figures dressed in military clothing have been seen throughout the building. Many people believe that General Patterson is one of the ghosts along with his son, Francis E.

Patterson. Francis was a brigadier general in the Civil War but was relieved of command in 1862 after an unauthorized withdrawal at Catlett's Station. Before an inquiry into the matter could be made, Francis was found dead from a gunshot wound in his tent. Whether it was accidental or intentional was never been determined. His funeral was held in the Patterson Mansion.

Most ghostly phenomena at the site are attributed to Albert Joseph Edmunds. Edmunds worked for the Society as a cataloger from 1891 to 1936. He loved his position so much that he told employees at the Society that he would never leave. Upon his death, his entire collection of writings was donated to the Historical Society and is housed in the fourth-floor vault. Edmunds described the location as "the ground floor of Hell."

Rolph states that typing is frequently heard on the third floor where Edmunds's office used to be. Another time, an address-label machine started working on its own. When an employee went to investigate, he discovered that it wasn't even plugged in.

Another employee opened a door and felt like she hit something. When she peeked around the door to see what she hit, she saw a black figure. Terrified, the woman ran out of the building and quit shortly thereafter. Another employee left after he experienced a ghostly event on the third floor one night. He never explained exactly what it was that happened.

ACADEMY OF MUSIC
240 SOUTH BROAD STREET

Obviously, the oldest opera house in the United States has to have a phantom. And the Academy of Music in Philadelphia has at least one that likes to guarantee that you never have to go to the theater alone. Patrons who happen to have an empty seat next to them have reported seeing the seat slowly depress, followed by squeaking as if someone sat next to them and is getting comfortable. This phenomenon is followed by a pinch or a hair tug, if the person next to the ghost happens to be a woman. During the show, a black figure can be seen lurking behind the final row of seats in the upper balcony. But he always disappears when the lights go up.

INN PHILADELPHIA / DELTA PHI EPSILON
251 SOUTH CAMAC STREET

If your name is George Lutz, be careful when purchasing real estate with a tragic history, or you may risk being haunted. At least that is the trend in New England. First it happened when a George Lutz purchased a house in Amityville, New York (or so he claims). Then it happened in Philadelphia when a (different) George Lutz purchased a building on Camac Street with his partner Phil Orchowski in 1993. The building had been unoccupied since 1987 after a disastrous fire destroyed the Deux Cheminées. The restaurant reopened a year later down the street.

Almost immediately the new owners experienced unexplainable phenomena. Three weeks before the opening of the new restaurant, Inn Philadelphia, Lutz was in the building alone when he heard footsteps walking above him. Fearing an intruder, he called his partner to come down to check things out with him. The two found no one in the building.

A few days later, workmen were on a coffee break at 7:30 a.m. when they heard voices on the second floor, followed by a crash. The men rushed upstairs to ensure everyone was all right. They discovered a large painting in the hallway. Somehow the painting had flown across the room and smashed into the wall with enough force to damage a freshly painted wall, but no one was on the second floor at the time.

The building was part of twelve row houses built in 1825. They were eventually transformed into six double-wide private clubs. Through the years the building housed a number of private clubs and restaurants, including the Poor Richard's Club. Rumors say the tunnel running underneath the 200 block of Camac was once part of the Underground Railroad, but this has never been proven.

As time went on, more and more people at Inn Philadelphia experienced the ghosts. The prep cooks refused to leave the kitchen when they were in the building alone because they heard voices and other sounds on the second floor. Other staff members reported hearing doors opening and closing, or voices coming from unoccupied areas of the building. And then there were the continual reports of the distinctive sound of step-drag footsteps.

According to Lutz, a few months after opening, the previous owner, Fritz Blank, came for a visit. He told Lutz that when they were preparing to open the Deux Cheminées in 1979 his father helped him renovate the building. His father loved carpentry and formed a real connection to the building. He also walked with a distinct limp. Sadly, his father had died shortly before the restaurant opened. It appeared his ghost was still looking over the building.

But while that explained the footsteps, Blank's father didn't seem the type to do some of the more "prankish" activity in the restaurant. After all, he loved the building, and wouldn't want to scare people. But not all the ghosts felt the same way.

In October 1995, a bartender and the night manager were closing. The bartender went upstairs to one of the dining rooms when he heard the door to the ladies room clang shut, although no one else should have been in the building. He went downstairs to find the manager, but when they arrived in the Franklin Room they saw the two grand chandeliers rotate wildly, stop suddenly, and then rotate in the opposite direction.

The two grown men fled to what they assumed would be safety. After all, the hauntings occurred on the second floor, not the first. Oh, were they wrong. Suddenly, music filled the building. Somehow the sound system, which had been off, had turned itself on and the volume up. The two men had enough. Without bothering to finish their duties, they turned off the sound system and lights, secured the building, and left.

Then there was the night a woman patron dining in the Green Room complained that someone kept pulling her hair. She and her husband assumed one of the servers was the guilty party and complained to Lutz. As they were talking to him, the woman's head jerked back and she cried out. Her hair had been pulled again, but no one was close enough to do it.

On another occasion the ghosts did not appreciate the performance of a New Orleans singer at a party. As she performed, items the staff needed disappeared. Then, three plates shot off a stack and smashed against the wall.

Some people claimed to see the ghosts. Often they would claim to see a shadow moving about the room. In addition, in April 1996 eight people waiting in the bar witnessed a "ghostly man" walk out of the coat-check room, pass across the bar, and then fade into the wall near the piano.

When Lutz investigated the hauntings, he discovered he was not the first resident to experience them. The previous owners admitted that they had also experienced the ghosts. Perhaps that was why the Deux Cheminées chose to reopen a half-block away after the fire.

The Inn Philadelphia has since closed and was purchased in 2006. The purchase was good for the building, bad for ghost hunters. The new owners did extensive renovations and restorations on the interior and exterior of the building, which is currently known as the Acanthus Building. After owning it for a few years, they sold it to the Delta Phi Epsilon, a sorority, which made the building its international headquarters. When contacted, a spokesperson with Delta Phi Epsilon said they were unaware of any "issues" with the building.

MCGILLIN'S OLD ALE HOUSE
1310 DRURY STREET

McGillin's Old Ale House is known as the oldest continuously operating tavern in Philadelphia. And what tavern would be complete without a couple of ghosts? The tavern is haunted by its founders, William and Catherine McGillin, better known as Pa and Ma McGillin. William McGillin founded the bar in 1860 at 1310 Drury Street. The couple lived above it and raised thirteen children. When William passed away in 1901, Catherine took over running the bar. According to her obituary, she locked the door of the ale house the day the 18th amendment became effective. She transformed it into a restaurant for the next thirteen years and then reopened it as a tavern when prohibition ended. She died four years later in 1937 at the age of ninety.

Many people at McGillin's believe that the spirits of both Ma and Pa McGillin still roam their beloved establishment. A manager reported feeling the presence of Ma on the first floor, and a spirit dressed in white was photographed in the mirror over the fireplace during a paranormal investigation. She doesn't seem to like the decorations in the bar, since the owner reports that they are constantly falling for no reason. Pa McGillin haunts the kitchen, perhaps because he died there. Employee Jim Pappas has seen a shadowy figure dart across the kitchen and observed pots fall off of the racks.

DRAKE TOWER
1512 Spruce Street

The Drake Tower doesn't look very spooky, until you notice how much it resembles Dana Barrett's apartment building in the movie *Ghostbusters*. The building used in the film is located at 55 Central Park West, in New York City. However, the Drake Tower was used for some of the exterior shots of the movie. Today the tower is an apartment building, but it was built in 1929 as a luxury hotel. Residents of the tower have reported seeing 1930s-era parties, as if they are looking through a portal to the past.

Part Three

NORTHEAST PHILADELPHIA

Northeast Philadelphia is a large section of the city inhabited primarily by European immigrants. The City Planning Commission divided the Northeast into two regions at Cottman Avenue: "Far Northeast" and "Near Northeast," although everyone usually substitutes "Lower" for "Near." Kensington is also considered part of Northeast Philadelphia.

The most notorious location in this area would have to be Byberry Mental Hospital. Although every effort has been made to erase it from the landscape, the stain of its past remains (along with its ghosts). Two other haunted hospitals are also located in Northeast Philadelphia, as well as a Civil War Museum that comes complete with several ghosts and a horse head. (No Civil War Museum is complete without a horse head.)

Chapter 12

Northeast
Hospitals

What is it about hospitals in Northeast Philly that makes them ghost magnets? One has a tragic history, while the other two have more benevolent ghosts who continue to watch over the hospitals they cared about in their lives.

BYBERRY MENTAL HOSPITAL
SOUTHAMPTON AND CARTER ROADS

An unwritten paranormal rule exists that any abandoned mental hospital must be haunted. Among the more famous haunted abandoned asylums include Waverly Hills, Trans-Allegheny Lunatic Asylum, Danvers State Hospital, Trenton State Hospital, and Pennhurst Asylum. The Philadelphia State Hospital at Byberry is not as well-known, but its history is just as horrific.

Better known as Byberry Mental Hospital or simply Byberry, it opened in 1903. It expanded through the years and by the 1960s it was the largest state hospital in Pennsylvania, with more than 7,000 patients. Unfortunately, Byberry did more mistreating than treatments. In March 1929, a patient died five days after his release. His family claimed he had been severely beaten before his release, but the coroner never investigated. In 1932, at least two patients committed suicide; one was thirteen years old. In

1970, an article in the *Philadelphia Inquirer* listed all the suspicious deaths reported at Byberry. A number of patients were beaten to death by other patients. Patients were tremendously creative in the tools they used to beat other patients to death. Iron bars, shoes, bricks, a broomstick, a wrench, and a chair were used when fists and feet didn't do the job.

The staff could be as deadly as the patients. On October 18, 1940, William Williamson was beaten to death by two attendants, who were later convicted of involuntary manslaughter. In March 1941, another patient, John Smith, was fatally beaten by an attendant.

Escapes from Byberry were also common, some with tragic outcomes. Patients would disappear for days, weeks, or even years before their bodies were discovered. Sometimes, they didn't travel far. Evelyn Griffith was discovered in a tunnel underneath the hospital in November 1942. She had been missing for a month. On June 24, 1947, the "badly decomposed" remains of Raymond McDonald were found in high bushes behind one of the buildings at Byberry. He had been missing for two weeks. In July 1970, two bodies were found. The first was the skeleton of a man found in tall weeds that hadn't been mowed in three years. No identification was made of the remains. A few days later, the decomposed body of Thomas Mulligan was found in a field of blackberries behind the hospital.

Patients who made it off the grounds didn't fare much better. On October 27, 1956, the skeletal remains of Helene Permanesk were found in the woods three miles from the hospital four months after she had gone missing. In 1965, patient Thomas Hanstein was struck by a freight train near the hospital after wandering off. On February 17, 1968, the partially burned body of Theresa Macutkiewicz was found in the bathroom at a Bensalem gas station two days after she went missing.

One of the more grisly tales is said to have occurred in June 1987, when a young woman at the hospital was raped and murdered by Charles Gable. The two were locked in a ward with forty other patients at the time. Gable then dismembered her body and escaped the hospital. The body (or rather body parts) of the female patient was not found for nine weeks, during which time the parts were used as playthings, one patient even showing off the woman's teeth.

While the Gable story sounds convincing, scouring the Internet and newspaper archives revealed no reputable source for the information. Considering that a month earlier (May 1987), Governor Bob Casey had commissioned a panel to investigate the hospital, the events should have come to light. As a result of the investigation, Casey ordered the hospital closed in December 1987 because of the poor treatment of patients.

Byberry's closure in 1990 began its journey into the ghostly legend. At first, the plan was to demolish the multitude of buildings. Asbestos scrapped that plan, since its removal would cost around $16 million, not including demolition. The state decided to leave the buildings intact and hire a security company.

The new plan was not without costs. Once Byberry had a problem keeping people in, but now it couldn't keep them out. After the body of a drug overdose victim was found inside one of the buildings, the state boarded up the doors and windows at a cost of $100,000. Nevertheless, the homeless, vandals, and "scrappers" continued to sneak into and damage the buildings. It seemed nothing the police did would keep them out.

The more derelict the buildings and overgrown the landscape became, the more the ghostly legends grew. Noises were heard coming from the "abandoned" buildings and attributed to the many ghosts haunting the grounds. People believed the ghosts of patients mistreated at Byberry had returned to haunt the grounds.

After years of abandonment, it was decided that the buildings had to go. But Byberry wouldn't go without a fight or claiming one last victim. On February 17, 2005, an inspector for LVI Environmental Services was checking the grounds for demolition. A stairway gave out and he fell two floors to his death.

The last derelict buildings were destroyed in March 2006. This hasn't destroyed the legend of Byberry. According to rumors, a former patient still haunts the underground catacomb-like tunnels that connected the buildings. Violent and psychopathic, he waits for hapless victims to wander beneath and slices the throat of anyone who crosses his path. Perhaps the legendary Charles Gable found his way back to Byberry? Another legend says that a Satanic cult opened a doorway to Hell on the grounds and causes the haunting. Those few who manage to find the entrance to the catacombs and venture inside run out in tears. (Since this is now private property, they should save those tears for when they get arrested for trespassing.)

Not all of Byberry was demolished. Self Help Movement, Inc. renovated a few of the buildings in the 1970s to help people with drug and alcohol addictions. They eventually took over several of the buildings at Byberry, which they continue to use. In fact, shortly after Byberry closed, a radio station held a haunted house at the site and donated the profits to the organization.

FRIENDS HOSPITAL
4641 ROOSEVELT BOULEVARD

Working third shift as a hospital security guard can be boring. The patients are asleep, the doctors are not making rounds, and everything stays quiet except for a few humming machines and the whispers of nurses.

So Dwayne* was surprised to hear a woman laughing as he made his rounds. Eager to talk to another person, if only in passing, he went in the direction of the sound, but no one else was around.

He mentioned it later to another security guard. Dwayne's tale didn't surprise the guard. He had a few unexplained experiences of his own. Like the night he was alone on the third floor and felt an icy hand on his shoulder. When he turned around, no one was there. He had also seen doors opening and closing by themselves. Then there's the phantom woman seen roaming the halls of Friends Hospital that resembles the wife of a former superintendent.

The Quakers founded Friends Hospital in 1813 as The Asylum for Persons Deprived of the Use of Their Reason. It was one of the first non-state hospitals for the sole purpose of providing treatment for the mentally ill. It also promoted humane care and treatment. Although in those days "humane treatment" meant bloodletting, purging, and spinning a patient around in a chair, that was still better than locking the

*Not his real name

person in the basement, which was usually the other option for dealing with mentally ill family members. The hospital later changed its name to the Frankford Asylum for the Insane and then to simply the Friends Hospital.

Roughly a dozen superintendents have served at the hospital since it opened in 1817. Dr. Edward Taylor was the head of the hospital from 1826 until 1832, when the doctor decided to retire. On March 23, 1832, he and his wife, Sarah, were climbing into the carriage to leave when she suffered a massive stroke. She was quickly carried into the hospital and died. Perhaps the thought of leaving her former home was too much for her and that's why she has never left.

But another possible source exists for the haunting. In late July 1906, Laura Hammel committed suicide by hanging herself at the hospital. According to a newspaper article, she had been given some yarn and knitting needles which she used to crochet a rope. She had been admitted for "suicidal mania" but no one imagined that she would knit herself to death. Could Laura be the cause of some of the hauntings?

The tunnels running underneath the hospital are also supposed to be haunted. The tunnels connect the buildings so patients and staff don't have to venture outside to go from one building to the other. But before the Civil War, the tunnels were also a stop on the Underground Railroad.

Only a portion of the original tunnels are still used. Moaning and other noises are often heard coming from the unused tunnels. For some reason, no one wants to investigate the dark tunnels for the cause of the sounds. One reporter for the *Philadelphia Inquirer* decided to brave them, but his flashlight died on him. He crawled back to the entrance in the dark.

JEANES HOSPITAL
7600 Central Avenue

Jane Brogan had worked the night shift plenty of times, but on this Friday night she was falling asleep. She needed caffeine, but the only vending machines were on the first floor. That meant she'd have to venture past the tunnel entrance, which always gave her the creeps. Her need for caffeine surpassed her fear.

According to Brogan's blog posting on OpenSalon.com, "I was heading to the cafeteria when out of the corner of my eye, I saw a woman dressed in head to toe black. She was maybe twenty feet away in the tunnel."

Since an elevator near the tunnel entrance went to the maternity ward, Brogan assumed the woman was on her way to visit a patient, and didn't think much about it. After getting her soda, she returned down the hall when she noticed the elevator to the maternity ward was still on the first floor. The elevator was old and notoriously slow. If someone had used it, it couldn't have returned back to the first floor in the brief time she had been at the vending machine. So where did the woman go?

Brogan hastened toward her own elevator that would return her to the third floor when a chill passed over her. She turned around and there was the woman. "She was about twenty feet away from me again, but at the entrance of the tunnel," Brogan wrote.

Brogan ran to her elevator. When she returned to the third floor, she was visibly shaken, which prompted a coworker to ask her what was wrong. Brogan described the woman in black, trying to convince both her and the coworker that it was just a late visitor.

"It wasn't a family member," the coworker assured her. She pointed to a portrait in the hospital. "Was that the woman you saw?"

Brogan looked at the black and white picture. Sure enough, it was the same white-haired lady dressed in a black dress that she'd seen on the first floor. Then she noticed the plaque that identified the woman: Anna T. Jeanes. Jeanes was the founder of the hospital and had died in 1907, more than one hundred years before.

Brogan wasn't the first person at Jeanes Hospital to see Anna. Others have also reported seeing an elderly woman dressed in black in or near the tunnel. A provision in her will had founded the hospital, and she had maintained a home on the grounds.

According to legend, Jeanes appeared to the hospital administrators in the 1940s. The hospital was in financial trouble and was considering a buyout offer. Like Bob Marley in Charles Dickens' *A Christmas Carol*, Jeanes returned to let them know they were going down the wrong path. The buyout never occurred.

Chapter 13

Civil War Museums

Civil War battlefields are notorious for being haunted. Civil War museums are not as common. Philadelphia had the distinction of having two haunted Civil War museums at one time, although only one is currently open to the public. But don't think that the ghosts in the museum are all connected to the building, because they are not.

GRAND ARMY OF THE REPUBLIC MUSEUM AND LIBRARY
4278 GRISCOM STREET

If you take a job working at the Grand Army of the Republic Museum and Library, be warned. They like to send new people to the basement in a bizarre hazing ritual. The veteran employees want to see how the new employees handle the ghost, just one of several living here.

Down in the basement, an angry spirit some call Phillip hides out. Visitors report feeling a negative presence that makes them sick to their stomach. It also drains the batteries of electronic devices. According to Dave Juliano, an investigator with Northeast Paranormal Association (NEPA), the male spirit likes to call people "colorful names." No one who visits the basement has had a positive experience with him. Electronic Voice Phenomena (EVP) sessions done here repeatedly recorded a voice saying, "Get out."

The Grand Army of the Republic Museum and Library, or GAR Museum, is a treasure trove of Civil War artifacts. Handcuffs found in John Wilkes Booth's suitcase, cannonballs embedded in tree trunks from the Battle of Chickamauga, canvas shoes found at Gettysburg, and even a horse head call this place home.

The museum is located in the historically registered Ruan House, constructed in 1796 by physician John Ruan. Although only 35 by 40 feet, the two-and-a-half-story building was considered large in its day. John and his new wife, Elizabeth Gibbs Ruan, moved in. They had three children while living there; two of the children died as toddlers in 1802, and Elizabeth died the following year.

Although John moved on, eventually marrying two more times before his death, Elizabeth still lingers in the attic of the house. A ghost investigator encountered her spirit there. When asked why she remained in the building, Elizabeth reportedly explained that she had died young and knew her husband had remarried.

On the second floor, the spirit of a young girl named Holly likes to hide under the table. Legend says that a child dashed in front of a carriage and was killed in front of the house when it was used as a kindergarten in the early 1900s.

Another female spirit has been encountered on the spiral staircase. She brings with her the strong scent of lilacs and taps guests on the chest if they complain they can't smell her. She is believed to have been a nurse during the Civil War.

In other areas of the house, shadowy figures walk around. Volunteers and visitors at the site have reported hearing loud, unexplained crashes; objects moving on their own; and lights turning themselves on and off. EVP sessions have reportedly recorded ghostly voices saying "Help me" and "What's that?" Photographs taken at the museum often reveal ghostly orbs.

A ghostly black cat also appears around the museum. Usually seen in the basement or on the second floor, according to museum archivist Kathleen Smith, the cat dashes in the back door in the basement and then vanishes.

An infamous item in the museum is not linked to any of the hauntings, but ironically almost started its own civil war: the mounted head of "Old Baldy."

Old Baldy was the favorite horse of Civil War General George Gordon Meade. Distinguished by the large white blaze on his face, the horse carried the general through several battles. During his service the horse was wounded several times, starting with the First Battle of Bull Run. At Antietam, he was wounded in the neck and left for dead, but was found grazing nearby after the battle was over and returned to service. At Gettysburg, the horse was shot in the stomach and Meade sent him away to recuperate. Baldy returned to service in 1864, but retired after being wounded by a shell at Weldon Railroad.

After the war, Old Baldy reunited with Meade in Philadelphia, and the two often took rides together through Fairmount Park. When Meade passed away, Old Baldy walked in Meade's funeral procession to Laurel Hill as the "riderless horse." The horse lived another ten years before dying of old age.

After he died (and was buried), someone decided to dig the horse up and preserve his head for posterity. The head was eventually given to the Grand Army of the Republic

Should Be Haunted: Mütter Museum and Museum of Mourning Art

19 South Twenty-Second Street and 2900 State Road in Drexel Hill

How can the Mütter Museum—which has a book bound in human skin, several thousand body parts, a collection of deformed babies, and an "adopt a skull" program—not have a few ghosts? (Seriously, for $200—which pays for cleaning, restoring, and remounting the skull—a plaque with your name will be placed next to your adopted skull.) The museum's website says it all: disturbingly informed.

While visitors can browse the collection of over 25,000 anatomical specimens, models, and medical instruments, they must be satisfied with a different type of dead since no ghosts have ever been reported here. One can only assume that even ghosts have limits.

Another museum that should be haunted (but for some odd reason is not) is the Museum of Mourning Art. Because of their interest in colonial America, the owners of the Arlington Cemetery in Drexel Hill started collecting art and objects related to funerals and mourning, mostly from the seventeenth and eighteenth centuries. In the 1980s, they built a replica of Mount Vernon, George Washington's Virginia home, for their office and filled it with their intriguing collection.

The museum is located on the edge of Arlington Cemetery (the PA one, not the DC one). The most unusual artifact would be the cemetery gun. Rigged to go off if someone tripped over it, the gun would protect graves from thieves—usually doctors and artists who wanted to study them. The gun was eventually outlawed after it claimed too many innocent victims (better known as mourners).

Museum and Library. In 1979, the museum lent the head to the Civil War Museum on Pine Street, because the Pine Street museum helped pay for restoration necessary to preserve Old Baldy. When the Pine Street museum closed in 2008, arrangements were made to display their collection—including Old Baldy—in other Civil War museums outside Philadelphia. But the GAC museum wanted the horse head back. A legal battle followed, obviously, because no Civil War collection can be considered complete without a horse's head. The GAC museum won and Old Baldy remains (or is it Old Baldy's remains?) at the museum.

CIVIL WAR & UNDERGROUND RAILROAD MUSEUM OF PHILADELPHIA
1805 PINE STREET

It's hard to interrupt a compelling card game—at least that's what curators at the Civil War & Underground Railroad Museum of Philadelphia learned. A group of Civil War–era soldiers were often seen playing cards in the Lincoln room, which was located on the second floor. The distinct odor of cigar smoke was also commonly smelled in the room. The haunting was featured on an episode of *Unsolved Mysteries*.

Phantom footsteps, cold spots, and an "eerie presence" were also experienced in the building. The museum closed on August 2, 2008. Most of its collection is being stored at the Gettysburg Museum and Visitor Center until a new site is established. Some artifacts are being displayed at the National Museum of American Jewish History on Independence Mall and at the African American Museum on Arch Street. There is no word about whether the ghosts moved with the collection or if they remain at 1805 Pine Street.

Part Four

NORTH PHILADELPHIA

North Philly is home to the city's most notorious haunted location, Eastern State Penitentiary. While some might claim it to be the most haunted location in Philadelphia, there are a few locations that give it a run for its money. One such site would be Fairmount Park, which has eight different locations that claim to be haunted.

Chapter 14

Fairmount Park

Located on both sides of the Schuylkill River, Fairmount Park is the largest landscape park in the United States at 4,180 acres. One could probably say it is the most haunted park, since eight locations within its grounds are considered haunted. Some of its ghosts even relocated here from other places.

PHILADELPHIA ZOO
3400 WEST GIRARD AVENUE

Primate keeper Desiree Haneman was walking toward the Penrose Building around 10 p.m. when she noticed a woman standing in a second-floor window. "I looked up into what was the library and there was a woman who had long blond hair," Haneman explained. Puzzled, since she didn't recognize the woman and it was late to have any special guests at the zoo, she took a better look. What she witnessed next terrified her.

"All of a sudden she had a kind of white light around her and as soon as we locked eyes she started to slowly back away from the window. At which point I freaked out and ran down toward the hippos to exit."

Haneman wasn't the only person to have an experience in the Penrose Building. Chief Operation Officer Andy Baker was walking toward the Penrose Building when he noticed the lights switch off. He figured someone was leaving, but no one came out of the building. Upon entering, he discovered the building was empty, although anyone exiting the building would have passed right by him.

For years, hauntings at America's first zoo were a closely guarded secret among its staff until one of them decided to contact The Atlantic Paranormal Society (TAPS) to investigate for their show *Ghost Hunters*. Only then did staff members relate the numerous paranormal experiences they have had at the Philadelphia Zoo. It seems the facility houses almost as many ghosts as it does animals.

The Philadelphia Zoo was chartered in 1859, but the Civil War delayed its opening by several years. The zoo opened its gates on July 1, 1874. Three thousand people visited the zoo that day. Admission was a mere 25 cents.

The land chosen for the zoo once belonged to John Penn, William's grandson. John had built a summer home, The Solitude, here in 1784. The building still stands on the zoo grounds and originally housed reptiles at the zoo. In this building, people have reported seeing a woman in a long dress standing at the top of the stairs or descending the staircase. The attic light is also seen turning on and off even though no one is inside the building at the time.

In the basement of the building is an old tunnel that used to connect the house to the kitchen that is used for storage. Board member Jody Lewis was in the area with her daughters when she saw a "misty white figure." Lewis paused and then turned to get a better look, but the figure was gone.

Across the park in the Treehouse, people have seen an apparition walk across the building. Others have reported hearing footsteps and feeling uneasy as if someone is watching them. This building was originally the antelope building, built in 1877.

The Shelly building is near the entrance of the zoo and houses the most dangerous animals in the zoo: the administrators. An employee working the switchboard saw curtains moving near one of the windows and a face peering out. Doors have also opened and closed on their own here, something Jason Hawes and Grant Wilson experienced here during the TAPS investigation. They both heard a metal door open and close, although no one else was in the building and they could not find the source for the sound.

Other people have reported experiencing intense chills and hearing disembodied voices in the zoo. Rumor says the zoo was built on a Native American burial ground. Archaeological evidence shows the Lenape established several villages along the Schuylkill River, and their customs included burying their dead. But no one has ever reported seeing a ghostly Native American on the site. (The Amityville House also attributed its hauntings to it being buried on an Indian burial ground; however, the claim was false.)

SIDE HAUNTS: PHILADELPHIA ZOO

The second-oldest zoo, the Cincinnati Zoo, also claims to be haunted by a ghostly lioness who stalks her human prey through the zoo. People have reported hearing soft footsteps and growls behind them but, just when they feel they are about to be devoured, the ghost disappears.

CEDAR GROVE MANSION
1 CEDAR GROVE DRIVE

Usually, ghosts connect themselves to a piece of property. If their original home is demolished, they move into the next building placed on that site. Sometimes ghosts connect themselves to an object. At Cedar Grove Mansion, the ghost connected itself to the house itself. When the house moved, the ghost went with it.

Elizabeth Coates Paschall built Cedar Grove Mansion in Frankford in 1746 on fifteen acres next to her father's house. Her husband, Joseph, had died four years earlier, but she continued to manage his business and their house in the city on her own. Cedar Grove was a rural retreat a few miles northeast of the city where she could get away. When Paschall died in 1795, the property passed to her granddaughter, Sarah. Sarah and her husband, Isaac Morris, enlarged the house considerably before passing it on to their son, Isaac, in the 1840s. He passed the house on to his daughter, Lydia Thompson Morris, who occupied the house until 1888, before she moved to Compton.

By this time, the area around the house switched from rural to industrial. Like her great-great-grandmother, Lydia loved Cedar Grove and hated the thought of it sitting empty or—even worse—being demolished to make way for more industry. She decided that she would save the house by moving it to Fairmount Park. Starting in 1926, she spent two years documenting and dismantling the house and then reconstructing it in Fairmount Park. Then, she gave the house to the city of Philadelphia. The Philadelphia Museum of Art currently uses the house as a historical showcase.

While many believe that Lydia wanted to save her family's beloved house, she may have been aiming at preserving something more: the two ghosts who call it home. Unless moving the house stirred up the spirits, Lydia likely had known about their presence in the house since one had been there since it was built. The original Grand Dame of Cedar Grove Mansion appears to live in her home. Her spirit has been seen peering out the fan-shaped window on the third floor.

Visitors and workers also report hearing disembodied whispering, giggling, and footsteps coming from the second floor. But this is not Elizabeth, but rather Sally Apthorp, a charming and accomplished woman. How do we know that she was charming? That's what is etched in one of the window panes: "Charming and accomplished Sally Apthorp from Boston Born 1760."

Sally Apthorp could be Sarah Wentworth Apthorp Morton, born in Boston in 1759. Sally was originally a nickname for Sarah in the 1700s. Sarah was an early American poet whose work received a lot of praise during her lifetime. Unfortunately, her talents were overlooked by her husband, who had an affair with Sarah's younger sister, Fanny, in their home. The affair resulted in the birth of a child and caused Fanny to commit suicide.

Although Sarah's husband, Perez Morton, was implicated by a jury in Fanny's death, his friends James Bowdoin and John Adams (yes, the second President of the United States) defended him in the *Massachusetts Centinel* on October 7, 1788. Perez Morton suffered no ill will from the events. He was elected to the Massachusetts House of Representatives and later became Speaker of the House. He even reconciled with Sarah. If the ghost is Sarah, no one could blame her for returning to Cedar Grove to relive a time before the tragic events in her life.

LEMON HILL MANSION
SEDGLEY & LEMON HILL DRIVES

Perched atop a hill overlooking the Schuylkill River, Lemon Hill is an idyllic place for picnics, bike riding, and other leisure activities. Even the hauntings are somewhat benign and less creepy than the usual hauntings. Well, most of them are.

The property belonged to Robert Morris, a close friend of George Washington who helped finance the Revolutionary War. Unfortunately, he overextended himself and was sent to debtors' prison in 1798. The property was put up in a sheriff's sale and purchased by Henry Pratt, who built the mansion which still stands on the hill. Pratt also built a large greenhouse and gardens that contained classical statues, fish ponds, and grottoes. For the next forty years, Pratt amassed a substantial collection of plants—nearly 3,000. Among them were several large lemon trees, which is how the house got its name. Amazingly, he never lived at Lemon Hill. He stayed in a townhouse on North Front Street and used the house as a retreat.

In 1836, for some unknown reason Pratt sold Lemon Hill. It could be that he felt he had no one to leave the property to since he had outlived his three wives and thirteen of his fifteen children. He died two years later on February 6, 1838. A few months later, on June 5, his entire botanical collection—including the lemon trees—was sold at auction.

For the next few years, the property went through various owners until 1844 when it was purchased by the city of Philadelphia. The city bought properties along the Schuylkill River to protect their water supply from industrial pollution.

The lemon trees are long gone, but their memory remains. Visitors frequently report smelling lemons and seeing ghostly gardeners lovingly tending their leafy charges. Henry Pratt's presence has also been felt in the house. Medium Marisa Pell visited the mansion for CBS Philly in 2010 and reported that Pratt still lingers at the house to ensure that it is looked after.

But another more mysterious ghost has been seen there on at least one occasion. In the 1990s, two Philadelphia police officers watched a woman dressed in white cross the road in front of them. She appeared to be walking from the Lemon Hill mansion and heading toward the river. Concerned that she was contemplating suicide, the two officers called after her. When she didn't respond, they climbed out of their cruiser and went in pursuit. But before they could catch up to her, she vanished before their eyes.

MOUNT PLEASANT
MOUNT PLEASANT DRIVE WEST OF RESERVOIR DRIVE

One winter, right before Christmas, a young girl was walking the grounds when a one-armed man suddenly appeared ten feet away from her. Frightened, she ran toward the house to find her mother, who was in the entry hall of Mount Pleasant. As the girl told her mother about the man, she suddenly let out a scream and pointed at a picture on the wall. "That's him," she told her mother. The portrait was of Captain John McPherson, who had been dead for 200 years.

Mount Pleasant was built on a hill overlooking the Schuylkill River in the early 1760s by Captain John MacPherson. MacPherson was a Scottish sea captain who worked as a privateer (or pirate depending on who tells the story) in the West Indies. He waged war against the French and Spanish in the West Indies from 1757 until the treaty between England, France, and Spain at Fontainebleau on November 3, 1762.

John Adams described him in his diary: "He has been nine times wounded in battle. An old Sea Commander, made a fortune by privateering. An Arm twice shot off, shot thro [sic] the leg." (Author's note: Adams never explains how one arm can be shot off twice. Seems to me that if it had been shot off the first time, it wouldn't be there to be shot off a second time. Whatever happened, MacPherson only lost one of his arms.)

His privateering days over, MacPherson decided to build the Palladian mansion. Its similarity to the Cliveden Mansion on Germantown Avenue is likely because both houses were based on British pattern books of that era. McPherson and his wife entertained the elite of Philadelphia, and their guest lists read like a who's who of Philadelphia at the time. John Adams visited the house on numerous occasions and described it as "the most elegant seat in Pennsylvania."

MacPherson sold the mansion on March 22, 1779, to Benedict Arnold, who gave it to his wife as a wedding gift. However, when Arnold defected to the British in September 1780, the property was confiscated. For the next few decades, the house changed owners until the city of Philadelphia purchased it in 1869. The city made it into a dairy farm to provide fresh milk and ice cream to children in the city.

MacPherson moved on in life, but he returned after his death in 1792. Visitors and employees of the house continue to see the figure of a one-armed man walking the property and the house. But he is not the only ghost in the house.

According to an article about the house in *National Magazine* published in 1913, Benedict Arnold also haunts the house. His ghost was seen "pacing the ancient floors with heavy tread and glowering fiercely at those who have encountered him during his ghostly visitations."

But the most bizarre ghost story is told by a security guard. He reported seeing a pair of red slippers on the steps of the house. He thought they had been left by mistake until he noticed the slippers moving down the steps as if being worn by invisible feet. Could it be the wife of either McPherson or Arnold returning to her former home? Only the shoes know for sure.

RODIN MUSEUM
2151 BENJAMIN FRANKLIN PARKWAY

The Rodin Museum has its own set of spectral lovers who haunt the gardens. They are seen sitting on one of the benches embracing before suddenly disappearing. They are the ghosts of tragic lovers Rachel and Hank.

Rachel was the youngest daughter of a prominent Rittenhouse Square doctor. Hank was a poor boy who lived in Brewerytown, a section of north Philadelphia. The two met in the Rodin Museum gardens and bonded over their mutual love of art. They spent many afternoons together at the museum.

When Rachel's father learned of the romance, he sent Rachel to school in upstate New York and then to Europe during her summer breaks. The two tried to keep in touch, but their efforts failed. For two years, Rachel was kept away from Philadelphia and Hank. When she returned, she discovered Hank's house boarded up. A neighbor informed her that Hank had been drafted to fight in the Vietnam War and had been killed shortly after his arrival. His mother died soon after, brokenhearted from losing her only child.

Shattered, Rachel stumbled back toward the bench behind the Rodin Museum where she and Hank met. But it was late so the museum was closed and the garden locked. In her frustration and grief, Rachel dashed across the busy Ben Franklin Parkway and was struck by a car. She died instantly. Although separated in life, the lovebirds are reunited after death at the Rodin Museum.

The story's details make it sound credible, but a search for historical proof turned up no documentation. Five Philadelphians named Henry died in Vietnam. The obituary of one of them, Henry T., lists his address as North Thirty-Second Street, which places it in Brewerytown. But it also says that he was part of a large family, not an only child, and that he enlisted, and wasn't drafted. Also, nothing suggests that Henry T. ever went by the nickname Hank.

The details of the other four Henrys match the story even less. None of them lived in Brewerytown or went by the name Hank. Perhaps the man's name wasn't Hank, but 641 other Philadelphians died during the war, according to the Philadelphia Vietnam War Memorial. And if his name isn't correct, who knows what else in the story is incorrect. No record of Rachel's death could be found, either.

FAIRMOUNT WATER WORKS
WATERWORKS DRIVE AND KELLY DRIVE

Fairmount Water Works was Philadelphia's second municipal waterworks when it was built in the early 1800s. Its architecture and engineering made it a popular tourist attraction, even drawing in Charles Dickens and Edgar Allan Poe. Poe described it as "wondrous to behold," which may be why he still lingers there. His ghost has been seen walking around here on several occasions. Sightings describe him as moving erratically and looking troubled and upset. Ben Franklin's ghost has also been seen strolling here, although it was built long after he had passed.

PHILADELPHIA MUSEUM OF ART
2600 BENJAMIN FRANKLIN PARKWAY

You don't have to have seen *Rocky* to recognize the Philadelphia Museum of Art; it was also featured in *Rocky II, Rocky III, Rocky V,* and *Rocky Balboa.* (The steps must have been sick or unavailable during the filming of *Rocky IV.*) After you finish dancing in a circle while humming "Gonna Fly Now" at the top of the steps, make your way inside, where you are sure to see a ghost.

"Ghost" is the title of Alexander Calder's sculpture seen hanging in the Great Stair Hall Balcony. This ghost is far more visible than all others in this book as it is thirty-four feet long. It is also the nicer of the two ghosts reported to reside inside this museum.

The other ghost has made one recorded appearance, according to Cynthia Bracelin in *Philadelphia's Haunted*

Should Be Haunted: Joan of Arc Statue

Kelly Drive and 25th Street

Close to the Philadelphia Museum of Art is the Joan of Arc statue, known as Jeanne d'Arc or in Philly as "Joannie on a Pony." It is a copy of the statue Emmanuel Frémiet sculpted for the French Republic's first president, Napoleon III. The model for the statue was an eighteen-year-old peasant girl named Aimée Girod who lived in Domrémy, Joan of Arc's village in France. In a tragic ironic twist, Girod burned to death in a fire in May 1937, just as Joan of Arc did in 1431.

Historic Walking Tour. In December 1997, a German tourist reported that she was slapped while walking through the Elizabeth Room. When they checked the security footage to see who had slapped her, they discovered no one (that they could see) near her. However, her face contorts as her neck snaps back as if she had been hit.

SIDE HAUNTS: BELMONT MANSION/BELMONT HOUSE

The rumors of Belmont Mansion ghosts are simply misidentification. In Dennis William Hauk's book *Haunted Places: The National Directory,* he lists the Belmont House at 511 Winding Way, Merion Station, as haunted. Some people have taken that information and applied it to the Belmont Mansion at 2000 Belmont Mansion Drive.

The Belmont House (a private residence) is said to be haunted by the apparition of a young woman who is wearing dark clothing and ascends the staircase next to the third-floor bedroom. She may be left there from when the house was used as a bordello (which has not been historically proven).

The Belmont Mansion, which currently houses the Underground Railroad Museum, is said to be haunted by its former owner Judge Richard Peters. CBS Philly did a "Haunted Philly Week" in 2010, during which medium Marisa Pell visited various historical locations, including Belmont Mansion. Both Pell and one of the workers at the mansion felt the presence of Peters, but no other ghostly activity has been reported there.

Chapter 15

Eastern State Penitentiary

Eastern State Penitentiary has been a legendary building in Philadelphia for almost 190 years. During its 150 years as a prison, more than one thousand inmates died within its walls. A few of them never left but wander the grounds as shadowy forms, making it a popular location for ghost hunters. Its website says it "may now be the most carefully studied building in the United States."

EASTERN STATE PENITENTIARY
2027 FAIRMOUNT AVENUE

No book on Philadelphia ghosts would be complete without a chapter on Eastern State Penitentiary. If Ben Franklin is Philadelphia's most famous historical figure, Eastern State Penitentiary (ESP) is its most famously haunted place. It is notoriously haunted, to the point where the real ghost stories have been stretched and elaborated until they barely resemble their original form. A good example of this is the story of Gary Johnson's experience at the prison. Johnson was a locksmith hired in the 1990s to do some restoration work at the prison. His experience is one of the first and the most famous recorded sightings at the prison.

In an October 24, 2013, NPR.org article questioning if ESP is haunted, Johnson's experience is recounted: "He had just opened an old lock in Cellblock 4 when he says a force gripped him so tightly that he was unable to move. He described a negative, horrible energy that exploded out of the cell. He said tormented faces appeared on the cell walls and that one form in particular beckoned to him."

An article on TravelChannel.com described Johnson's experience differently. It says, "He saw several ghosts and felt a cold hand reaching into his body. Johnson said he was almost certain that the ghosts were going to kill him."

Similar versions of these stories are published on websites and in books, but none of them claim to have interviewed Johnson or explain where their version of the tale originated. This is disturbing since the story differs from the one Johnson himself told in an interview that is part of a 2000 television program titled *Night Visitors*.

In the video, Johnson describes his experience by saying, "I had this feeling I was being watched, real intensely. And I turn and I'm looking down the block and I know there's nobody there. A couple seconds later I get the same feeling: I'm really being watched. And I turn and I look down the block and I don't see anything and as I start to turn back to the block, this black shadow just leaped across the block."

While it is possible the show edited Johnson's story, it seems strange that they would cut out the best part, given that the images and music being played in the background were designed to enhance the creepiness. It is also possible Johnson has told different versions of his story through the years.

Johnson was also interviewed for an episode of *Ghost Hunters* in 2004. During that show, he pointed to a "little wall" outside of the prison where he claimed a figure appeared, which suggests he wasn't even in a cellblock at the time of his sighting.

Another possibility is the story has been distorted through various retellings, like what happens in the game of "Telephone." Some people may have even deliberately distorted the story in order to make the haunting claims more legitimate. This seems even more likely when you consider that some sites claim that Johnson's work on the lock opened a spiritual gateway in the prison that allows the spirits to roam freely.

Paranormal reality shows have had a major effect on ESP as it is a favorite location. Just a few of the shows that have featured ESP are *American Paranormal, Ghost Adventures, Ghost Hunters Academy, Haunted Encounters, Haunted History, Most Haunted Live! USA, Mysterious Worlds, MTV's Fear, Paranormal Challenge, Scared!, Scariest Places on Earth,* and *Weird US. Ghost Hunters* liked it so well they went twice.

While this is great publicity for ESP, it creates a lot of controversy. TV shows want to create an exciting show and rarely care about accuracy. Many have been accused of either manufacturing evidence or misrepresenting experiences had by investigators. Although the paranormal investigators might go to the location with the best intentions, those involved with producing the show tend to promote the show in such a way as to increase ratings.

Locations can also get wrapped up in their own publicity as they learn that, in the twenty-first century, ghost tourism means money. In 2015, ESP charged groups $25 an hour per person (with a minimum of $500 per group) to do a paranormal investigation. ESP's website claims about sixty paranormal groups visit each year, which brought at least $30,000 in revenue.

Ghosts appear to be a controversial topic at Eastern State. Their site says simply, "Many people believe that

Eastern State Penitentiary is haunted." And while many staff members have gone on record saying that they believe it is haunted, at least two former tour guides have publically proclaimed it is not. In a 2013 interview with NPR, tour guide Ben Bookman claimed most people who worked at the facility did not believe in ghosts. "It's a lot harder to find a believer than it is to find a skeptic here. We at Eastern State do not claim that the prison is haunted."

But just as an atheist in the congregation isn't enough to disprove a religion, having employees who don't believe in ghosts doesn't disprove whether a site is haunted. A wise woman once said, "There are two types of people: those who believe in ghosts and those who haven't had an experience with them yet." (Author's note: Okay, the wise woman was actually me. I often said this to unbelievers during my days working as a historical ghost tour guide.)

Another reason could exist for the skepticism tour guides have. Some feel talking about the ghosts takes away from the actual history and real people who lived and died there. Luckily, most ghost hunters know that you can't understand the ghosts until you understand the history.

In 1787, a group of Philadelphians met in the home of Benjamin Franklin to discuss the problem with public prisons. In the late eighteenth century, prisons were simply holding pens where men, women, and children were housed together. Prisoners were subject to all sorts of abuse, from both the guards and their fellow prisoners. Dr. Benjamin Rush proposed a unique idea: a system that would generate change in criminals and not just punish them.

Thirty years later, the Commonwealth of Pennsylvania decided to build such a place on farmland just outside Philadelphia. Eastern State Penitentiary opened in 1829, the most expensive building in America at the time. It was built around a Quaker-inspired system that believed isolation, introspection, and work would push inhabitants toward spiritual reflection and cause them to change.

Each inmate was given a private cell that included central heat, running water, a flush toilet, and a skylight. At the time, not even the White House included those luxuries. The prisoners were isolated at all times. When out of their cell, they were required to wear hoods. Talking was strictly forbidden. It was believed that the prisoners, alone with their thoughts, would see the errors of their ways and repent.

And while ESP intended to do away with the cruelty of other prisons, it failed miserably. On the outside, it was marveled for its design and intentions. It became a tourist attraction in Philadelphia almost immediately. People came to study it, and its design was the basis for at least 300 other prisons around the world.

But some who came saw more than officials intended. Author Charles Dickens wrote in his travel journal, *American Notes for General Circulation,* about his own visit to ESP:

> In its intention I am well convinced that it is kind, humane, and meant for reformation; but I am persuaded that those who designed this system of Prison Discipline, and those benevolent gentleman who carry it into execution, do not know what it is that they are doing. . . . I hold this slow and daily tampering with the mysteries of the brain to be im-

measurably worse than any torture of the body; and because its ghastly signs and tokens are not so palpable to the eye, . . . and it extorts few cries that human ears can hear; therefore I the more denounce it, as a secret punishment in which slumbering humanity is not roused up to stay.

Those in charge of the prison did not agree with Dickens, and became quite forceful in the means they used to ensure the inmates followed the rules. While the system did instill changes in the inmates, it wasn't changes that were intended. Inmates went insane and died—some at their own hand—as a result of their treatment at ESP.

By 1913, the "Pennsylvania System" was abandoned and ESP was transformed into a regular prison. But reformation wasn't enough to save the prison. By the 1960s, the prison was in need of serious repairs that it couldn't afford. The state decided it would be cheaper to close the prison, which it did in 1971.

The facility spent the next twenty years being neglected and vandalized until 1991, when a generous donation from The Pew Charitable Trusts allowed preservation efforts to begin. The same year, the first fund-raiser on Halloween took place. The event eventually turned into the Terror Behind the Walls, one of the largest and most successful "haunted" attractions in the country.

The Pennsylvania Prison Society finally opened for historic tours in 1994. Visitors were required to wear hard hats and sign liability waivers before the tour. (The waivers were required until 2008.) Eventually, the Eastern State Penitentiary Historic Site, Inc., a nonprofit organization, was created to preserve the site and operate the tours.

One of ESP's most notorious inmates was Al Capone, although he wasn't there for long. On May 16, 1929, Capone and his bodyguard, Frank Cline, were arrested outside the Stanley Theatre in Philadelphia for carrying a concealed, deadly weapon. At 11:30 the following morning, the two were placed on trial. They pled guilty and were sentenced to a year in prison. They were originally sent to Homesburg Prison, but Capone was transferred to Eastern State Penitentiary on August 8, 1929, where he finished out his sentence. (Cline was transferred to ESP about a month later.) The men were released two months early due to "good behavior" on March 17, 1930.

Capone's arrest came four months after the St. Valentine's Day Massacre, the name given for the murder of seven men associated with the North Side Irish gang. Although Capone was never convicted of the crime, most people believe that he ordered the murders in a failed attempt to take out Bugs Moran, Capone's rival and the leader of the gang.

Inmates at ESP reported that Capone was often heard screaming at night and begging for "Jimmy" to get out and leave him alone. One of the victims of the massacre was Albert Kachellek, who had changed his name to James Clark to protect his family from being related to a Moran gangster, but went by the name Jimmy. Those visiting ESP today won't run into Jimmy's ghost, however. He continued to haunt Capone until he finally passed away in 1947.

Keep in mind that no one knows for sure which cell was actually Capone's during his stay. All anyone knows is that he stayed in the "Park Avenue" section of the prison, but even the location of that section can't be proven.

Although Al and Jimmy may not be haunting Eastern State, there are plenty of other former inmates who have decided to linger for reasons unknown. According to Brett Bertolino, ESP Program Coordinator, "There have definitely been times where I heard something—something that sounds like footsteps—or you see a shadow. Usually I'm alone and usually I didn't stay long enough to find out what it was."

Two lone beings are most commonly seen in the prison. The first is known as the "solitary figure." A black, human-like ghost stands quietly until someone gets too close, and then it darts away, leaving a feeling of anger and malevolence in its wake. This ghost stays primarily in the older cellblocks. The other is a silhouette of a man seen in a guard tower, believed to be the ghost of a former guard who stayed after death to watch over the prison.

A few specific locations have become famous for being "more haunted." In Cellblock 4, ghostly faces of former inmates are said to float through the cells. In Cellblock 6, shadows dart across corridors, move along the walls, and disappear into the cells.

A ghost dog has been seen and heard throughout the prison. Many claim to have seen the ghost of Pep. Pep was a black lab who was allegedly sentenced to life for murdering a cat. The dog actually belonged to Governor Gifford Pinchot, who donated the dog to the prison in an attempt to improve conditions in the prison. However, Pep was only at the prison for five years before he was transferred to the recently built Graterford Penitentiary. Through the years other dogs were kept at the prison,

Should Be Haunted:
Penn Mutual Life Building

520-540 Walnut Street

Before Eastern State Penitentiary was built, prisoners were sent to the Walnut Street Gaol (Jail), built between 1773 and 1776. Conditions here were atrocious. Prisoners were confined together regardless of age or sex, resulting in disease and rape. Jailors focused on selling their prisoners alcohol, food, clothing, and heat rather than protecting their prisoners from each other. Many incarcerated here died from starvation or exposure. The conditions eventually improved after a group of citizens formed the Philadelphia Society for Alleviating the Miseries of Public Prisons. The prison closed and was demolished in 1835, shortly after Eastern State Penitentiary opened. The Penn Mutual Life Building was erected on this site in 1930, but sadly no ghosts have moved in.

including a beagle that belonged to the captain of the guards in the 1950s.

That may explain why Emily Bittenbender, president of the penitentiary's board of directors, saw not one but two dogs. "I've had a few personal experiences, . . ." she said. "The most significant was when I saw two ghost dogs in Cellblock 12."

And it is Cellblock 12 that appears to have the most reported sightings. A high-pitched cackling laughter has been heard repeatedly there, along with faint voices. Tour guides report seeing all the iron doors on the third floor of the cellblock closed, only to discover them open moments later. Black shadowy figures have also been seen walking on the catwalks. According to Bertolino, "Several people have told me that in Cellblock 12 on the second floor at the very end they have seen a shadowy figure come out of the cell on the right and just stand in the hallway."

Alaina Mabaso, a former tour guide at ESP for three years, gave a behind-the-scenes look at what might be causing some of the hauntings in her self-titled blog in 2012:

Those who heard bangs and rattling chains in CB 4 were actually hearing large, chain-mounted signage, invisible in the dark, stirring in the breeze. The footsteps in Cell Block Two were actually a steady chorus of drips in an old laundry facility that was perpetually flooded. An inexplicable whoosh in front of your face was a close encounter with one of the prison's bats. The whispers in the dark were actually bits of plaster crumbling to the floor, as if exhausted by the day's heat. The glowing orbs captured on camera in Cell Block 12 were a 40-year case of rampant dust reflecting the flash.

But even Mabaso, who doesn't believe in the ghosts, had at least one experience she couldn't explain. She had led a tour outside Cellblock 2 when one of them took a picture of the prison's east side. In the picture "was a perfect, life-sized, transparent silhouette of a person in what had definitely been a deserted frame. I could see the outline of a head, neck, shoulders and torso as if someone were standing a few feet from the camera. The scenery the photographer had wanted to capture was visible through the body." Mabaso has been unable to find any non-supernatural cause for that photograph.

Mabaso's blog also gives an insight as to the effect that paranormal shows have had on the penitentiary. She talks about how Cellblock 4 became known as "Dude Run," referring to an incident that occurred during *Ghost Hunter's* first visit.

During the first night of shooting, Brian Harnois and Dave Hobbs spooked themselves in Cellblock 12. After taking a picture, Hobbs claimed to have seen a black image. One of them screamed, "Dude, run!" and the two grown men raced down the corridor. (Apparently, it was slightly more manly to run in terror then it was to pee your pants, but by only by a slight margin.) Both men were chastised severely by TAPS founders Jason Hawes and Grant Wilson. Wilson said it best: "You want to investigate the paranormal but you're freaking terrified of the paranormal? I don't understand the logic."

After the show aired, tourists visiting the prison filmed themselves recreating the event, yelling, "Dude, run!" But this wasn't the only notorious event that occurred during the filming. There is also the footage caught in Cellblock 12 of a black-cloaked figure racing down the corridor toward the camera. A few feet before it reaches the camera, it changes direction and disappears into the dark.

The footage was instantly caught in the Catch-22 of all ghost pictures. If the footage is too poor, it is dismissed as your eyes playing tricks on you. If it is too good, people say it was a hoax. This footage landed almost in the center. While it was clearly a cloaked figure running down the corridor, the footage wasn't quite clear enough to rule out a possible hoax.

Even Hawes and Wilson felt the footage required more investigation before they determined its authenticity. They returned to ESP to attempt to debunk the image.

Unfortunately, their attempt to recreate and possibly debunk the image only created more controversy. They decided to have Brian Harnois cover himself with a dark blanket and run down the corridor. Harnois seemed like a good choice, since he had already demonstrated his ability to run in pitch-black darkness.

For some reason, this time Harnois hesitated. He shuffled his feet down the corridor, ignoring everyone's urging to run by complaining that he couldn't run because he couldn't see anything. Plus his image isn't even close to what was seen on the tape: The blanket failed to cover him completely and he is significantly taller than the image.

Critics point to TAPS's half-hearted attempt at recreating the footage as evidence that they were unwilling to admit that they could have been pranked. Some even suggest it as proof that TAPS was in on the fakery. It doesn't help that in their book *Ghost Hunting,* Hawes writes that Harnois "did his best to cooperate . . . but nothing in Brian's performance came close to replicating the image we had recorded."

The grainy footage provided in the episode is difficult to analyze, but a couple of things stand out that suggest it was a living figure. First, as the figure changes direction, part of the cloak changes color. Some suggest this might be a person's sneakers or pants leg. Also, a white object hanging from the ceiling swings harder as the figure passes, indicating air movement. Neither of these things should have happened unless the figure was solid.

In their book, Hawes gives additional (circumstantial) evidence to suggest it was hoaxed. They say the footage was shot while everyone was on a dinner break. That means everyone would be in one location, allowing someone to slip in, create the footage, and leave with no one being the wiser. Another group has attempted to recreate the footage, the Skeptical Analysis of the Paranormal Society, a (now-defunct) group created specifically to disprove evidence on *Ghost Hunters*. They were able to recreate the footage, but only if they recorded at fifteen frames per second and then played it back at thirty frames. This would mean that at least someone at TAPS would have to be in on the hoax.

It would be easy to point fingers at someone connected with the TV show or Eastern State because they have the most to gain from it. But they would also have the most to lose if a hoax was discovered. It could just as easily have been someone who thought it would be funny to get one over on a TV show. Interestingly, in the more than ten years since the episode aired no one has bothered to step forward and claim the hoax, including former employees who have been fired from the show.

Ghost Hunters returned to ESP during their second season. Again, they made no attempt to recreate the footage. It was almost as if their hearts weren't in it. After the night was over, they had nothing to broadcast. Apparently the ghosts didn't show up.

But no one has ever doubted the existence of the ghost cats loitering around ESP. Of course, these were not real ghosts or even real cats, but the title of a series of thirty-nine sculptures by artist Linda Brenner. The statues were a tribute to a colony of feral cats that occupied the prison after it closed, and to the man who took care of them.

Shortly after the prison closed in 1971, the city hired Dan McCloud as a groundskeeper. He was later reassigned, but he continued to stop by the prison at least three times a week to feed the cats. He did this for the next twenty-eight years. Every Monday, Wednesday, and Friday morning, he brought a gallon of water, a gallon of milk, and ten to twelve pounds of cat food for the cats.

Dan the Catman, as he was soon known, lived by a motto that he wrote on a piece of paper and taped on one of the feeding stations: "Take care of God's animals and He'll take care of you."

When Dan's wife died in 1993, four months short of their fiftieth wedding anniversary, one of the last things she asked him was, "Did you feed the cats today?" That same year, the Preservation Coalition of Greater Philadelphia took over the prison. They had the cats trapped, neutered, and then released. Dan continued to feed them until 1994. Eventually, the care of the few remaining cats was passed on to staff members at ESP.

Brenner's sculptures were placed around the prison in 2005. The number of sculptures was slowly reduced until there were only a dozen still on display in 2010. In 2012, the remaining ghost cats were removed from the exhibit.

Chapter 16

Around North and Northeast Philadelphia

Although the stories here don't have as much anecdotal evidence to back up their ghostly claims, they are still worth visiting. Some of the sites are long gone but their stories (and sometimes their ghosts) remain as a tribute to their Philadelphian past.

HAG OF PINE STREET

When walking on the south side of Pine Street be careful not to dawdle between Sixth and Seventh Streets, or you might face the "Hag of Pine Street" (also known as the "Witch of Pine Street"). Years ago, a particularly unpleasant woman lived on this street. Clearly, death has not improved her mood.

After her death, passersby would often see a pale, wrinkled face peering from the window of her now-empty house. Weird screams, muffled moans, shrieks, and groans were also reported from the site. But what made things worse is that the ghost didn't restrain itself to the house. Neighbors reported seeing a ghostly figure lurking in the shadows.

Not surprisingly, the house remained vacant for many years until a woman named Betsy Bassett bought it. According to Bassett, she drove the spirit from the house with the assistance of a Voodoo priest. Despite this, some locals still claim to hear strange noises coming from the area.

CHALKLEY HALL
Wheatsheaf Lane and Sepviva Street

The spirit of an unhappy young woman still haunts her old homestead. Legend says she is the daughter of Thomas Chalkley. She loved a young man who failed to win her family's approval. After her parents forced her to break off the relationship, the girl committed suicide and became the Gray Lady of Chalkley Hall.

The 1912 book *The Colonial Homes of Philadelphia and Its Neighbourhood* first mentions this ghost: "Like most old houses, Chalkley Hall has its ghost, and the Little Gray Lady appears now and again to warn of deaths and other momentous occurrences." A January 4, 1955, article in the *Evening Bulletin* gave a similar description when it said the ghost "floated about the old staircase whenever someone was about to die." A 1937 Philadelphia guidebook also mentioned that a ghost here liked to "hover in the night."

Chalkley Hall was demolished in 1955, despite its 228-year history, but that hasn't put the Gray Lady's spirit to rest. According to a local security guard, she still appears every now and again.

Author's Note: While researching this story, I came across a picture of Chalkley Hall on the Temple University website (at http://digital.library.temple.edu/cdm/search/searchterm/ P059099B). The photograph was dated between 1915 and 1935 and is of the front of the building. Clearly visible is the figure of a young boy wearing a white shirt and dark pants.

What's odd is the torso and head of the child are translucent but the legs are not. While figures can be made translucent if a photographer is using a long exposure, I've never seen it happen with only part of the figure before. Probably not a ghost, but fun to find while researching.

STANDARD TAP
901 NORTH SECOND STREET

Late one night, long after Standard Tap had locked its doors and sent its patrons home, a few employees remained in the building, cleaning and setting up for the next day. Finally, long after midnight, they were ready to go home. One of the barbacks (a bartender's assistant) had finished closing the second level when, halfway down the stairs, he remembered his iPod.

Rather than turn the lights on, he used the glow of various electronics to guide his way. He snatched up the device and turned to go downstairs when he saw her. Down the hallway toward the back dining room, next to the closet door, stood a gray-haired woman in a blue dress. At first, she looked normal, until she began floating above the floor.

He stood staring at her for a few moments before the shock cleared and he raced down the stairs. The woman has also been spotted at the top of the stairs on several occasions by another bartender and several customers.

But she's not the only ghost at the bar. A man dressed in a Civil War uniform has been seen standing outside the kitchen. And then there's Mr. Smeigelski, who lived above the tavern. He may have passed on, but he hasn't moved on.

Smeigelski could be classified as more poltergeist than ghost. He has knocked over shelves, turned on the water, emptied towel holders, and overturned bags. At least, that's what he does if he *likes* you, which hasn't always been the case.

Smeigelski took a disliking to a new employee, who was too dominant and always causing drama in the bar. Finally, Smeigelski had enough of him. One afternoon, this employee was setting up the kitchen when a utensil rack flew across the room. It hit the wall, barely missing the employee. Spoons, forks, and spatulas clanked against the tile floor. The employee freaked out and quit, much to Smeigelski's delight, since it was his last act of aggression.

ST. ANDREWS IN-THE-FIELD EPISCOPAL CHURCH
500 SOMERTON AVENUE

St. Andrews in-the-Field Episcopal Church doesn't have a cemetery or lengthy history like most churches in Philadelphia. They do have "hazy white figures" seen on the grounds of the church and "strange noises" from "the woods" nearby. Since "the woods" is a small patch of trees, this sounds more like an urban legend or at least an Internet one.

BRIGHT HOPE BAPTIST CHURCH
1601 NORTH TWELFTH STREET

Bright Hope Baptist Church is a "young" church by Philadelphia standards since it was built in 1964. It has an Internet reputation as haunted, which may or may not be true. Every site found listed the same comment about it: "Sounds of unsettlement have been heard behind the church after everyone leaves the building." The description makes it sound more like the church has a raccoon problem and not a spectral one.

ORLEANS 8 MOVIE THEATER
2247 BLEIGH AVENUE

Being scared wasn't restrained to horror movies at the Orleans 8 Movie Theater. A little girl haunted the movie theater. She was most often heard giggling and asking people to come play with her. Her identity was never known and, since the theater was closed in 2007 and then demolished, it will likely remain a mystery. A Target parking lot currently sits on the former theater location.

JAMES MARTIN SCHOOL
3380 RICHMOND STREET

Take a one-hundred-year-old building, make it into an alternative middle school, and add the rumor it was once a mental hospital, and you will get masses of urban legends and ghost stories. According to the stories, bloodied hands materialize on the walls and ghostly people appear in the mirrors at the school. People have also seen a face in the window of the blocked-off attic. The ghosts are said to be either:

1. boys who were cutting school, got trapped in the attic, and died;
2. a former mental patient who threw himself out of the attic window; or
3. several mental patients who went into the attic and slit each other's wrists.

Research doesn't lend any credibility to these stories, however. According to the Pennsylvania Historic Resource Survey Form submitted to the National Register of Historic Places, the building was built between 1894 and 1896 as a school. And while it became a nursing school in 1947, patients have never been housed there. In other words, any ghosts residing at 3380 Richmond Street are in the minds of its students.

Part Five

NORTHWEST PHILADELPHIA

Northwest Philadelphia wasn't always a part of Philadelphia. In the 1700s, the area was considered far enough outside of the city that it became a refuge for people trying to escape the yellow fever epidemics. But by the mid-1850s, the city had grown to the point where the area was enveloped and became part of Philly.

One of the defining moments in this area was the Battle of Germantown, when the British marched toward Philadelphia down Germantown Avenue. This area of town should be known for having quite a few haunted mansions. What's really unique is that most of these mansions have several ghosts. Apparently, people never want to leave this part of town.

Chapter 17
Battle of Germantown

Nothing like a good battle to create a few ghosts. And the Battle of Germantown during the Revolutionary War created quite a few of them, including two different headless ghosts!

September 1777 was a difficult time for the Revolutionaries. On September 11, General George Washington suffered defeat against British General Sir William Howe at the Battle of Brandywine Creek, which left Philadelphia vulnerable. On September 26, the British captured the city (then the nation's capital). Howe left three thousand troops in the city and took the remainder of his forces five miles northeast of the city to Germantown.

The division of Howe's forces gave Washington numerical superiority and he planned to use that to his advantage by attacking Howe's forces at Germantown. On October 4, 1777, the two forces met again.

Washington's plan was to sneak up on the British from four separate fronts in the middle of the night and attack. Unfortunately, the darkness combined with dense fog during the day created chaos and confusion. Soldiers got turned around, lost, and confused. By the end of the day, the Americans retreated after suffering over one thousand casualties, twice as many as the British.

Side Note: During the Battle of Germantown, General Howe suffered a personal loss. Somehow during the chaos of the battle, his dog went missing. Two days later, on October 6, 1777, the dog was returned to him with a note written by Alexander Hamilton that read: "General Washington's compliments to General Howe. He does himself the pleasure to return him a dog, which accidentally fell into his hands, and by the inscription on the collar appears to belong to General Howe." Apparently, Washington was compassionate to his enemy even in defeat.

GRUMBLETHORPE
5267 GERMANTOWN AVENUE

Grumblethorpe sounds like the name of a Harry Potter character. The name comes from a novel by Edward Nares about a German family in England, *Thinks-I-To-Myself*. Built in 1744 as a summer house by John Wister, Grumblethorpe was first called (predictably) John Wister's Big House until Charles Wister change its name in the 1800s.

In September 1777, the Wister family left Justinia (Justina) Hemberger, a young German servant, in charge of the home while they stayed in another home away from the British forces. Justinia had come to live with the Wister family as a child after her father, Justin, passed away. When the British occupied the city, General James Agnew decided to use Grumblethorpe as his personal residence and headquarters. Agnew had been wounded at the Battle of Brandywine Creek and was still recovering.

On October 4, 1777, Justinia was working in the garden when the battle began. Agnew quickly collected his horse and prepared to join the combat. He paused to warn Justinia of the dangers, but she disregarded his advice and continued working. Agnew turned his horse and continued on his way.

He didn't get far. Reports of what happened next differ. The accepted story in Germantown is that he was shot by a civilian sharpshooter, Hans Boyer, a short distance from the house. Afterwards, his men carried him back to the house and laid him on the floor of the parlor. The British won the battle, but Agnew didn't live to see it. He bled out, leaving a permanent bloodstain on the floorboards. He was buried in an unmarked grave in the De Benneville Family Burial Grounds.

When the Wisters returned, rather than replace the stained floorboards, they left them. They weren't troubled by the stain, since it was British blood. They also kept the hoe Justinia was using that morning as a memorial of the day.

Since that day, people report seeing a black mist rising from the bloodstained spot on the floor and roaming throughout the house. On one occasion, Diana Thompson, Education Director at Grumblethorpe, saw "a black shape, low to the ground, spinning very quickly from the dining room into the Colonial parlor." As soon as she said, "I'm not in the mood for this," the shape vanished.

Thompson didn't tell anyone what she had seen. A few days later, her son approached her and asked, "Mom, have you ever seen a black shape moving really fast?" He had seen the same thing.

Other staff members have reported seeing eyes or full-bodied figures in the dining room mirror. Legend says if you stand on the bloodstained spot on October 4, you will hear Agnew moaning just as he did many years ago.

Justinia also haunts her former home. Justinia loved to bake and would spend Friday nights baking bread to be distributed to the poor on Saturday morning. Late one night in 1820, the Wister girls reported seeing Justinia standing in their bedroom. This startled the girls because Justinia should have been in their home on Market Street, miles away. The following morning, the discovered that she had died the night before. That event marked the first encounter with Justinia. Her spirit is often encountered around sunset in the house, accompanied by the smell of freshly baked bread. On one occasion, volunteer Kelli Alsop was walking through the second floor of the house with Thompson and another woman. The sun was streaming through the windows. According to Alsop, "You could see the shadows on the floor. Behind me, there was another shadow and it was wearing a dress. But all of us were wearing jeans."

Although Alsop has not had any negative experiences with the ghosts, they have become a problem for her. One day her mother and cousin were sitting in their car outside the house waiting for Alsop when they felt the hair of the back of their necks stand up. Since then, her mother refuses to go near the house, which means Alsop has to arrange other means of transportation.

Grumblethorpe is currently open to the public. On display in the house, you will find a variety of items belonging to the Wister family, including Owen Wister's desk that he used when he wrote *The Virginian*.

CLIVEDEN MANOR
6401 GERMANTOWN AVENUE

American troops advancing down Germantown Road stumbled upon a British picket outpost near Allens Lane in Mount Airy. Artillery fire was exchanged, alerting British

Colonel Thomas Musgrave's 40th Regiment, which consisted of six companies (around 120 men). They had been camping in a field near Benjamin Chew's house, Cliveden. The soldiers at Allens Lane fell back and joined Musgrave. The Americans' advance unit chased after them, but passed Cliveden in the fog. Musgrave realized his troops were now cut off from the main British line and immediately ordered them into the mansion. He closed the first-floor shutters, barricaded the doors, and posted marksmen at the second- and third-floor windows.

The soldiers were then forced to wait for the Americans to attack. Musgrave warned his men that should the Americans gain entry to the house, they would all be put to death. Their situation—a few men defending a house against a large number—was grim at best. Tensions skyrocketed.

As the soldiers waited, they discovered an elderly woman hiding in the cellar of the house. Before they could decide what to do with her, one of Musgrave's soldiers cracked under the pressure. He severed the woman's head and raced around the grounds holding the severed head by its gray hair.

What happened to the woman's body (and head) afterwards is unknown, but apparently they were never reunited. Since that tragic day, visitors and residents to Cliveden report seeing the ghost of a headless woman wandering the grounds searching for her head.

When Washington and his troops reached the Chew House, British sniping from the second floors attracted their attention. Washington's first inclination was to bypass it. However, his artillery commander, Brigadier-General Knox, convinced him that they should not leave a British stronghold to their rear, and Lieutenant John Maxwell's brigade was ordered to capture the building. Maxwell's first action was to send Lt. Colonel William Smith with a flag of truce to Cliveden in the hopes of getting Musgrave to surrender. Smith was shot and later died from his wounds. Six cannons were brought in to bombard the building from both the front and rear. The cannonballs barely dented the stone walls, although they caused plenty of casualties when they overshot the house and landed on the other side and hit American troops. Grapeshot fired in the windows also had little effect.

Maxwell decided to launch a series of infantry attacks on the house. The few men that managed to get to the house were bayoneted when they tried to enter. The colonials tried to set the house on fire, but were unsuccessful.

Meanwhile, the attack on Cliveden drew the attention of American General Adam Stephen. He ordered his troops to double-back to provide support. In doing so, they passed behind General Anthony Wayne's soldiers. Convinced that the British were flanking him, he ordered his troops to fire. Stephen was forced to retreat.

After several futile hours, Maxwell admitted defeat and ordered his men to fall back. Their departure left fifty-three of his men dead on the grounds of Cliveden, four of which were on the front porch and eighteen in the driveway. How many Redcoats died during the siege is unclear.

It's also unclear what happened to the dead left by the retreating forces, but they may not have received a proper burial considering that many people say their ghosts continue to haunt the grounds. According to *Ancient and Modern Germantown,* an 1889 tome by Samuel Fitch Hotchkin,

Germantown residents "were afraid of the ghosts which were supposed to visit Chew's stone wall at night." When a man foolishly tried to promote the ghost stories by wrapping himself in a sheet or blanket and pretending to be the ghost, "men caught and flogged him."

Hotchkin's book also says that legend had it that, after the battle was over, a number of dead soldiers were cast into a well on the Cliveden property and that "their ghosts were naturally expected to appear." The well has disappeared, but it is believed to have been near the corner of Johnson Street and Germantown Avenue.

But rumors of Cliveden being haunted can be traced back to an 1841 article in *Graham's American Monthly Magazine of Literature, Art, and Fashion* titled "The Ghost of Chew's Wall." According to the article, several citizens saw the ghost on November 17 "perched upon Chew's Wall, dressed in white and rattling a heavy chain." They theorized the ghost was a British soldier who had deserted during the Revolutionary War. On October 4, 1777, he was being held prisoner in a baggage wagon and was either accidentally shot in the crossfire during the Battle of Germantown or murdered by "some enemy in his own ranks."

The ghost reappeared a week later, this time dressed in black and walking around on all fours "like a hyena." That night the ghost "throttled" a German man named Christopher "Stoffel" Burger. A group of townspeople met to discuss the problem and decided a committee consisting of eight men would go out and shoot the ghost with a silver bullet, which should make it disappear. Stoffel, since he had seen the ghost and would thus be able to point him out, was elected head of the committee. (After all, they didn't want to shoot the wrong ghost.)

The group went out the following night and "set up a terrible yelling, in order that the ghost might see that they were in earnest and prepare for the consequences." The article doesn't explain what exactly the men said, but whatever they did worked. The ghost appeared thirty yards away.

The men cocked their muskets and "poured a dreadful volley into the offender and took to their heels." In other words, they turned and ran like scared children once they were out of bullets. It wasn't until the following morning that anyone was brave enough to see if the committee was successful. Upon investigation, at least two silver balls were lodged in a fence post. Some suggested the committee had gotten drunk while preparing for their "ghost hunt" and fired directly at the post. However, the committee "unanimously agreed that if the ghost had stood where the post was, he would have had a ball through him to a certainty."

With that decision made, one would suspect they would have declared the ghost "dead" or rather "deader." But their actions did not get rid of the ghost. People continued to see the ghost on and around Chew's Wall after that. A 1914 book titled *Germantown Gardens and Gardners*, by Edwin Costley Jellett, mentions a ghost that "walked [Cliveden's] walls at the 'Curfew Hour.'" Although the definition of curfew hour varies, it is usually around 9 p.m.

Today Cliveden is a museum and is open for tours from April until December. Visitors may notice that museum staff often pronounce the name of the house CLIFF-den, but refer to the nearby street as CLEYVE-den, although the two are spelled the same way. An early letter found by the museum spelled the name Cliffden, which led them to believe that was how the name was pronounced. The house was named after an estate in Buckinghamshire, England.

ALLENS LANE

Sleepy Hollow, New York, may have its fictional headless horseman, but Philadelphia has a real one. Allens Lane is a road in Mount Airy that extends from Germantown Avenue to the Wissahickon Valley. On foggy nights, people report seeing a man dressed in Revolutionary War attire galloping down the street and carrying his head in front of him. He is believed to be a British soldier who lost his head during the Battle of Germantown. (Although, since he is holding his head, he technically didn't *lose* it. Maybe he can help the old woman at Cliveden find hers.) Apparently, he is attracted to men in uniform since the first reported sighting was by British soldiers during the Revolutionary War and the last documented sighting was in 1986, when he was seen by two Philadelphia police officers. Allens Lane has also been spelled Allen's Lane or Allen Lane.

Chapter 18

Driving Down Germantown Avenue

Germantown Avenue is a long stretch of road that goes through Germantown and connects Center City with Chestnut Hill. One of the most haunted locations on this stretch of road is Loudoun Mansion, where Maria and her brother Willie haunt. Then there's the lonely bridegroom who never got to marry his beloved, and the playful sprite, Emily.

LOUDOUN MANSION
4650 GERMANTOWN AVENUE

In June 1993, lightning struck Loudoun Mansion, causing a fire. Everyone assumed the worst. Things not destroyed in the fire were probably destroyed by water or smoke. And if it hadn't been for Maria Dickinson Logan, the 200-year-old antiques inside the home might have been destroyed. Logan is the former owner of the estate. She had passed the property over to Fairmount Park after she died . . . in 1939.

"Everything Maria liked and wanted was saved during the fire," Anita Feldman, a volunteer with Friends of Loudoun told a reporter with the *Philadelphia Daily News*. "All of the family portraits survived. Everything Maria loved survived. But her brother, Albanus, had some furniture that she hated and wanted him to get rid of. All that furniture was destroyed in the fire."

While that could simply be a coincidence, coincidence doesn't explain the sampler. As Feldman explained, "The firemen were amazed that the sampler sewed by Sarah Logan—it's one of the oldest samplers in America, from about 1725—wasn't touched by the fire. But the wallpaper all around the sampler was burned black."

Maria Logan is only one of several ghosts at Loudoun. Her will specified that she intended the property to be used "as a park for the use and enjoyment of the citizens of the community." And as a citizen of the community, she obviously feels she is entitled to use it herself.

According to Mrs. John Farr, head of the Friends of Loudoun, "Some of the neighbors say that Miss Logan is guarding the property. Children tell of seeing someone sitting on the sunporch, most often a little old lady. And I must say a number of things have happened for which there are no explanations."

Her spirit is felt most strongly in her room. A depression appears in her chaise lounge as if someone is sitting there. Her slippers and other belongings move about frequently, as if someone is still using them.

Anyone who is brave enough to spend the night in Maria's room risks being woken up by an elderly lady sitting on the end of the bed shaking her clenched fist. But who can blame her? What would you do if you discovered someone sleeping in your bed?

Maria was one of seven children born to Gustavus and Anna Armatt Logan. Two of the children died in infancy. Her sister, Jane, the only sibling to marry, moved to London with her husband. Her other sister, Fanny, joined Jane across the pond. Albanus, often called "Lo" and mentioned earlier, died in 1930. And then there was William, better known as "Willie."

Willie died on March 31, 1860, according to his mother's diary. He was only seven years old. (Sources have listed Willie's age as young as six and as old as eleven. However, at least two sources, one dated 1883 and the other 1911, state his date of birth as December 1, 1852.)

Not much is known about Willie, including his cause of death or even where he was buried. There is a rumor that he had an intellectual developmental disorder, which could explain why there is no real record of his life except for a couple of photographs.

Little Willie is described as a mischievous boy accompanied by a large dog. The spot near the chimney in the minister's room where Willie would be forced to stand as punishment is often colder than the rest of the room. People believe it is Willie's way of making his presence known. And given his behavior after death, he likely stood there quite often in his few years on Earth.

Willie is famous for pulling pranks. He likes to move objects around and hide them. One favorite target is a baby cap kept in a locked case. "If we put out a china display, they'll be soon packed up and put in boxes," Feldman said in a 1993 interview with the *Philadelphia Inquirer*.

On one occasion, committee members had spent several hours arranging heirloom Limoges China inside the china cupboard. As the hour was getting late, the members decided to quit work for the night and finish later. They carefully locked the cupboard before securing the house and leaving. When they returned several days later, they were shocked to find the cupboard empty. The only explanation they could discern was someone had broken in and stolen the china. But nothing else was missing and the doors were secure when they entered.

A few days later, a volunteer was on the second floor looking for something in a closet. Inside the closet was a high shelf that required a ladder to reach. She fetched the ladder from storage and continued her search. Although she didn't find what she was looking for, she did find the missing Limoges china! They blamed the incident on Willie.

On another occasion, Mrs. Farr was getting ready to leave when she discovered her purse had disappeared. She had left it in the drawing room. Thinking she had set it somewhere else, she searched the house, but couldn't find it. As it was quite large, it would have been hard to miss. Two days later she found the purse sitting in plain view in another area of the house, its contents intact.

Willie also likes to play with the books in the library. Usually, the books are organized in a particular order—at least they are until Willie decides to play. When workers arrive they find the books thrown around the floor, sometimes in patterns. Books have been found stacked on the floor as if someone used them to make a fort, or as stepping-stones around the room.

Willie apparently has enlisted a friend to haunt the house with him. A little girl approximately the same age as Willie and dressed in nineteenth-century clothing has been seen in the house. She enjoys romping around the corridor. Her identity is unknown and none of the house's former residents lost a female child at that age.

The Battle of Germantown occurred before Loudoun Mansion was built, but it still left its mark on the property. Loudoun was built in 1801 on Neglee's Hill, one of the highest hills overlooking Philadelphia. During the battle, wounded American soldiers were brought to the hill where the house now sits. A total of 152 American soldiers died at the Battle of Germantown. After the battle was over, the wounded were taken to the city, but it is unclear what happened to the dead. Some say they were buried where they died atop Neglee's Hill, which means the house was built over a cemetery.

This belief is strengthened by the sight of orbs and other lights moving through the grounds. But they don't restrain themselves to the grounds; they may also have taken up residence in the house. People frequently see lights moving through the house when it is supposed to be empty.

However, this could be the ghost of James Skeritt (Skerrett). Skeritt was the second husband of Jane Caroline Armatt, Maria Logan's grandmother. Skeritt spent a great deal of time and money fixing up the house. He is seen as a black shadowy figure walking up and down the staircase or standing on the second-floor landing.

A caretaker cleaning the house was startled to find a man dressed in black standing behind her. Before she could ask him who he was, he vanished. It is unclear if this ghost was Skeritt or one of the soldiers who died on the property.

Then there is the "mysterious force" that helped Anita when she lost her balance while going down the mansion's basement stairs. She is certain she would have fallen to her death had it not intervened.

Not everyone finds the ghosts amusing or enjoyable. A park historian was alone in the attic when he felt something hit his back. Perhaps Maria didn't want him to go through "her" things. A local neighborhood organization also stopped booking space at the mansion after unexplained voices and footsteps interrupted two meetings. And you thought having loud neighbors was bad!

DANIEL BILLMEYER HOUSE
6504 GERMANTOWN AVENUE

The footsteps of a ghostly bridegroom are heard walking quickly up the stairs of the Daniel Billmeyer house. But when he arrives at the top and discovers his bride is nowhere to be found, his footsteps are heard slowly descending the stairs in defeat.

In 1793, Philadelphians were leaving the city in droves, attempting to escape the yellow fever epidemic. Many relocated in Germantown, which wasn't part of the city at that time. Two such refugees were a young couple about to be married. Since space was at a premium, they rented rooms on the second floor of Daniel Billmeyer's recently renovated house. The original house had been built in 1730s, but

Michael Billmeyer expanded it in 1793 for his son and prospective daughter-in-law.

Sadly, the wedding never took place. According to the legend, the groom contracted yellow fever and died the night before his wedding was to take place. His spirit now remains in limbo since he wasn't able to marry his beloved. Any bride who spends the night here before her wedding will hear his footsteps climbing the stairs and making his way toward her bedroom.

According to one former owner, Manning Smith, in 1959 her daughter, Carol, spent the night before her wedding in the master bedroom and heard the footsteps running up the stairs. The event seemed to awaken the ghosts, according to interviews Smith gave the *Philadelphia Inquirer* in the 1960s.

Smith reported that several "mischievous, but very friendly" ghosts haunted the house. Besides walking up and down the stairs, the ghosts moved furniture around, hid important papers and items, and would create disorder in the house. "Some persons have suggested that I misplaced the things," Mrs. Smith explained, "but I know better. It's the poltergeists." (Author's note: based on that philosophy, my house is also haunted.)

Throughout the 1960s and 1970s, Smith frequently opened her house for tours and ghost hunts (for a small fee) and even invited more than one hundred experts on ESP to the house to investigate. The Gilberti family purchased the house in 2004. According to Christian Gilberti in a 2009 article, the ghosts came with the house. They still hear footsteps on the stairs and in the hallway. He also says that the heavy dining room door closes on its own.

CRESHEIM COTTAGE CAFÉ (AKA CANTINA AVENIDA)
7402 GERMANTOWN AVENUE

This restaurant on Germantown Avenue has long been known for poltergeist activity. Lights turn on by themselves, items disappear and reappear somewhere else, and the attic door opens and closes on its own. Everyone believes that the ghost responsible for these occurrences is that of a young girl named Emily. No one knows how old Emily is (or was) but she appears to be between nine and eleven years old. She has long, dark "Victorian-styled" hair and wears a pink dress with a satin bow. She is also shy, always vanishing within seconds of being spotted (although she has appeared in a couple of photographs), and usually appears on the second floor.

Emily's spirit emerged during renovations in 1996. Contractors reported seeing a "short shadow" on three different occasions that they believed to be a ghost.

Emily has been reported to play with the computer and thump on the wall. Former owner Kenneth Leger also recounted that people have seen shadows floating down the hallway and heard a child either crying or whispering. Leger owned it when it was known as the Cresheim Cottage Café, which closed around 2009.

In 2009, Edgar and Kim Alvarez re-opened the restaurant as Avenida. In newspaper interviews, Edgar claimed to have heard Emily closing doors upstairs late at night and making noises. She would also turn the music off. "Sometimes when we close, we stick around to do inventory and she turns the music off on us. Usually right around midnight. . . . It's like she's telling us to go home." The name of the restaurant was changed to Cantina Avenida in 2014, but the name change and Emily's presence wasn't enough to keep it going. It closed its doors in October 2014. Whether a new restaurant will open in this location remains unknown.

Chapter 19

Baleroy Mansion

At Baleroy Mansion, the question is not "Who haunts it?" but "Who doesn't haunt it?" At least eight ghosts prowl this house, although it is barely over one hundred years old (which by Philadelphia standards makes it the new kid on the block).

BALEROY MANSION
111 West Mermaid Lane

Baleroy is a thirty-two-room mansion built in 1911 and purchased by May Stevenson and Henrietta Easby in 1926. Henrietta was the granddaughter of General George Meade, the famed General of Gettysburg. The couple moved in along with their two sons, George Meade and May Stevenson Jr., better known as "Steven." The house may not have been haunted when they moved in, but it certainly became that way by the time they left—not that they all left.

The youngest and possibly first ghost at the mansion is that of Steven Easby, who died shortly after his family moved into the house. According to his brother George, one morning he and his brother were playing when they paused to look into the fountain. When Steven looked into the water, the reflection of his face was replaced with the image of a skull. A few weeks later, Steven contracted an illness and died. He was only eleven years old.

But George always felt Steven continued to haunt the residence, and he's quite the prankster. He is believed to have caused an antique pot to fly across the room and strike a respected minister.

One night during a dinner party, a loud crash was heard. When George and his guests investigated, they found a portrait of Steven fifteen feet from the wall where it had been hanging. The hook, however, was still firmly in the wall and the wire on the back of the portrait was intact. Workers at the house have reported seeing a young blond-haired boy in the window of the mansion. David Beltz was working on the back of the house when he saw what he described as "a young kid with blond hair. He had his hands on the sill and was looking down toward the yard." As he pointed the boy out to his coworker, the boy faded before their eyes. On another occasion, he and fellow contractor Eddie Robinson saw Steven on the main staircase. In an October 31, 1994, article in *People* magazine, Beltz said, "It drifted by the window. Then all of a sudden there was this cold vibration." Beltz also said he and fellow contractor Eddie Robinson have heard "unexplained footsteps and voices" while in the house.

On one occasion, a worker saw the boy disappear in front of his eyes. Shaken, he left and never returned to finish the job. Before he left, he described the ghost to George. His description matched that of Steven.

Another time, a worker and his son were both working in the house. While in the basement, the son heard his name being called several times. When he went to investigate, he found his father working in the attic and no one else in the house. The son refused to work in the basement alone after that.

Steven may also be the ghost who likes to play with electricity, which tends to go off for no reason—as does the alarm system. After a number of false alarms, the police started writing "ghosts" as the cause on their reports.

Thomas Jefferson's ghost has been seen in the dining room standing near a large grandfather clock. Although he died long before the house was built, Easby owned items that belonged to Jefferson, which could account for the sightings.

An elderly woman with a cane haunts the second floor. She is believed to be the first owner of the house and resentful of anyone else being in "her" home. She can be heard walking around, knocking on surfaces, and has even materialized to threaten visitors with her cane, only to suddenly vanish.

The most infamous ghostly resident of the house prefers the Blue Room. The room is an eighteenth-century drawing room, which contains secret compartments and, most notably, a blue "death chair" with a bone-chilling history. A "death chair" should be black and made of iron or steel, not blue and upholstered with large yellow and red flowers. But then you shouldn't judge a chair by its cover.

The chair is rumored to be at least 200 years old and have belonged to Napoleon Bonaparte, although the latter is probably not true. Easby did own a chair that belonged to Napoleon, but it was described as a "low red satin chair with the Napoleonic emblem" according to a July 26, 1991, article in the *Philadelphia Inquirer*.

More likely the chair belonged to the ghost said to haunt it, a woman known as Amelia or Amanda. When Amelia was present, a blue mist would form in the room (which is how the room got its name). Anyone who dared to sit in Amelia's chair in her presence would die—which happened to at least four people, including a former housekeeper, Meade's cousin, and a friend and employee named Paul Kimmons.

Kimmons was asked to escort psychic Judith Haimes through the house when he had his first sighting of Amelia floating down the stairway in the house. Before that, he had not believed in ghosts. But Amelia wasn't done scaring him. According to Haimes, Kimmons called her and told her that as he drove home from the mansion, he looked in his rear-view mirror and saw Amelia sitting in his back seat. When he turned around to get a better look, she disappeared. But every time he looked in the mirror, he could see her.

She tormented Kimmons by appearing everywhere he went. She would wake him in the middle of the night by standing over his bed. She would appear on the street when he would go shopping. Finally, an exhausted Kimmons was found slumped over in the Blue Room in Amelia's chair. He died shortly thereafter.

On another occasion, another friend of Meade's, Lloyd Gross, was helping prepare the mansion for a charity bene-fit. Gross noticed a "blue smoke" just beyond the Blue Room doors and mentioned to Easby that it must be getting cold because of the strange blue fog. Easby quickly corrected him: it wasn't fog, it was ectoplasm. Gross became unnerved and decided to go home. As he walked to his car, he turned and asked Easby why he had hit him. He realized, however, that Easby was too far away from him to have been the cul-prit. No one else was around. No one except perhaps Amelia, and she wasn't finished scaring him. When Gross arrived home, he saw smoke in the foyer and thought it was on fire. Then he recognized it as the same blue ectoplasm that he had seen at Baleroy. Amelia had followed him home. Gross must have made peace with her, however, because Amelia eventually left him alone.

George also blamed Amelia for waking him up one night by sitting on his bed and grabbing his arm so hard she left bruises. He switched on the light, but no one was there. He learned to keep Amelia's spirit appeased by draping a cord over her chair so no one would sit in it. He also avoided the Blue Room whenever she made her presence known.

George's mother also haunted Baleroy. According to Dolores Riccio in *Haunted Houses U.S.A.*, Easby often saw his mother walking around the house. Even Easby's father, who had never believed in ghosts, changed his tune. Shortly before his death, he told George that he had seen his wife's spirit in the house. Easby even found, with the help of his mother's ghost, a letter written by his father which said "I was brought up not to believe in ghosts and to trust only what science could explain, however I have seen the ghosts and there is no reason to be afraid."

In 1984, Gross was escorting Louis Gallo, a freelance reporter, through the house. They were in the East Room, Henrietta Easby's old bedroom, when Gallo's tape recorder flew out of his hand. The reporter claimed it had been pulled out of his hand. According to Easby, "I guess she didn't want it playing in her room.'" Easby took the reporter out to the balcony and gave him a scotch to calm his nerves. George also believed an uncle haunted the grounds, but never explained why he felt that way.

As if ghosts inside the house are not enough, a ghostly car haunts the driveway. People continually report hearing a car pull up the long driveway, only to find it empty when they check to see who arrived. Some even report seeing a long, black car similar to those found in the 1930s in the driveway, but it vanishes whenever they try to get a better look.

Before his death, Easby intended to make Baleroy a non-profit foundation and, since its residential location didn't make it a suitable site for a museum, use the site for historical research. Sadly, he passed away in December 2005 without any direct descendants. After a legal battle between relatives of Easby and Easby's domestic partner Robert Yrigoyen, the house was sold and the historical collection was sold at auction or donated to museums.

Easby swore he would join the ghosts after his death, but no one has reported seeing him since his death. Perhaps he is appeased since the new owners have made it a family home as his parents intended. They even have two boys.

The new owners have admitted to having at least one encounter with Steven. The couple was sitting with some close friends of theirs when the other couple saw a young boy walking through the hallway outside the living room. They immediately insisted on checking on the boys, both of whom were fast asleep. The other couple had no prior knowledge of the ghosts.

The scariest part of this story is what has happened to the blue chair and Amelia. No one knows, although the chair was likely auctioned after George's death and Amelia's spirit went with it. Hopefully, the new owners are giving Amelia the proper respect and the chair hasn't claimed a fifth life. But I would avoid sitting in any blue chairs with yellow flowers, just to be safe.

Part Six

WEST PHILADELPHIA

The boundaries of West Philadelphia have no real definition. For the purposes of this section, it includes all city land west of the Schuylkill River. That includes the area of University City, an area closest to the Schuylkill River that includes the University of Pennsylvania, Drexel University, and the University of the Sciences.

Will Smith called the West Philly neighborhood of Wynnefield home, which is why the title song of *The Fresh Prince of Bel-Air* says "In West Philadelphia, born and raised . . .". He's not the only royalty to come out of that city. Katie B. Jackson is known as the "Queen of Wynnefield" due to the influence she had on the community in the 1960s.

American Bandstand started out at WFIL-TV (now WPVI-TV) on Market Street. Rumor has it that Dick Clark saw the ghost of a coworker there. Clark was on his way to prepare for the show when he saw the man in the hallway. As the man had been terribly ill, Clark was surprised to see him and asked him how he was. A few days later, Clark learned that the man had passed away while in the operating room, at the same time Clark had seen him at the station.

Chapter 20

General Wayne Inn

The General Wayne Inn ghost stories have been told since 1848. While quite a few ghosts haunt the inn, including that of Edgar Allan Poe, the inn's namesake, General "Mad Anthony" Wayne, is far too busy to haunt it himself. Or maybe there is just not enough room at the inn for him.

GENERAL WAYNE INN
625 Montgomery Avenue, Merion Station

One afternoon Alice Gormley was setting up for dinner service at the General Wayne Inn when she heard someone call her name. Engrossed in her work, she ignored it. But the person repeated her name three more times. Exasperated, she stopped what she was doing and turned around. "What do you want?" Alice asked when she saw him.

"He was a man standing on the stairs, and he had this uniform on . . . a Revolutionary War soldier, only to me he was like a general. . . . And he looked so startled when I said, 'What is it?' And, just like that, he disappeared." Later the bartender took one look at her and said "What's the matter? You look like you saw a ghost."

"Well, I think I did," Alice replied.

The General Wayne Inn was built in 1704 by Robert Jones. He called it the Wayside Inn. Jones died in 1747 and Anthony Tunis rented the property and renamed it the Tunis Ordinary. The Tunis Ordinary also held a general store and a post office supervised by Ben Franklin, who had been appointed by King George III as Postmaster of the colonies.

Anthony Streeper purchased the property in May 1776. When the Revolutionary War began, he left his wife in charge of the inn and joined the Fourth Pennsylvania Regiment. The inn's location made it desirable to both the British and the Americans as a strategic command post. It changed hands a few times during the war. In 1795, the inn was renamed the General Wayne Inn, after General "Mad Anthony" Wayne who stayed overnight at the inn on September 13, 1777, and returned in 1795 to celebrate his successful Indian campaign. That name stuck and is still visible on the side of the building today.

The first recorded sighting of a ghost at the inn occurred in 1848 when it was a polling center. A woman went down to the basement to get some additional ballots. When she returned, she claimed to have seen a soldier dressed in a green uniform. People continued to see this soldier, always in the basement, and usually near the wine cellar. He was described as wearing a green uniform with a yellowish lapel and sporting a black moustache. This description matches the traditional uniform worn by Hessians during the Revolutionary War.

The basement-dwelling Hessian origin has a number of legends. A popular tale is that, while Americans controlled the inn, they dug a tunnel from the basement that led to either a nearby field or the blacksmith shop across the street. One night, when the inn was controlled by Hessians, a young soldier sent into the basement for more wine stumbled across Patriots smuggling supplies through the tunnel. To prevent him from exposing them, they killed the Hessian and buried his body in the tunnel. Others say the Hessian had been hiding in the basement and was killed by either Mrs. Streeper or soldiers.

Most of the ghostly activity recorded at the inn was during the time Bart Johnson owned it from 1970 until he retired in November 1995. In 1985, Johnson was approached by a part-time contractor named Mike Benio. Benio claimed that every morning at 2 a.m. a ghost came into his bedroom, sat on his bed, and woke him up. The ghost introduced himself as Ludwig and claimed he had been killed during the Revolutionary War and was buried in the basement of an "old inn" in Merion.

Benio decided it must be the General Wayne Inn and asked for permission to dig in the basement to look for the bones. Amazingly, Johnson agreed. Benio dug for two days but stopped because his efforts were weakening the foundation of the inn. Benio did discover an old root cellar, some broken pottery, and a few bones. But it was never determined whether the bones were human.

The Hessian isn't the only soldier at the General Wayne. Another two ghostly soldiers are looking for things they lost. The first, known as Willem, was a Hessian that was either killed during battle or wounded by Patriots while on a midnight walk around the property. His commander, noticing that the man's uniform and boots were still in good condition, stripped him and buried him in his underwear.

Willem is trying to find his clothing so he can be buried properly.

The other is a British soldier who was wounded nearby and brought into the inn. He died before telling anyone who he was. The only identifying feature was a locket that contained a miniature of a young woman. The soldier was buried in the Stranger's Yard next door to the inn, but the locket was put on display at the inn with the hopes that someone would be able to identify it and the soldier. Unfortunately, he was never identified and is agitated about not having his locket. He appears in the inn and demands his locket back.

Another psychic reported to the *Philadelphia Inquirer* in 1992 that a Hessian soldier named Paul also haunted the inn. Paul had been taken from his farm and forced into military service. He fell in love with a barmaid at the inn and decided to desert. He was found and executed for desertion, and is buried in an unmarked grave on the property. Paul might be the Hessian who hid in the basement, or they could be two separate ghosts.

Workers and guests have seen the soldiers in almost every room of the building and on the grounds. Usually, they are full-bodied apparitions, but not always. Sometimes they are only heard. One night, a waiter in the bar described hearing footsteps "as if somebody was walking down the entire length of the bar, all the way down." He never saw anyone, but patrons sitting on the bar stools felt the boards moving as the footsteps passed by.

Dave Rogers, a maître d' at the restaurant from 1974 until 1980, was closing up one night when he saw a head sitting on the bread drawer in the kitchen. "And it was a very smoky color, as if it was a projection onto a screen or something," Rogers described. "[It] had a very painful expression . . . thin, black, slicked-back hair. His ears stuck out a little bit. He had pencil thin eyebrows and a pencil thin mustache. And no neck or anything, just—just a head. He was just sitting there, looking at me."

Why just the head? The ghost may have been playfully pranking him, a common occurrence here. Johnson described one of the pranks to the show *Unsolved Mysteries*. On busy nights in the bar, it was common for the girls to sit on the bar stools while their male companions stood behind them. "And at ten, eleven o'clock at night one of our entities . . . will go down and . . . blow on the back of a [girl's] neck," Johnson said. "The girl would immediately whip around and ask, 'What did you do that for?'"

The ghost repeated the pattern with the next girl, then the next, all the way down the bar. "I would purposely position myself so I could see if it was going to happen again—this blowing on the back of the girls' necks scene. Because it's a funny scene. I knew when the first one started that it would continue all the way down to the end of the bar. It always did."

The ghosts also moved things around. One night, Johnson and a waiter were on the second floor when they heard loud noises above them. They hurried upstairs and discovered chairs and tables overturned in the locker room outside the third-floor office. But no one had been on the third floor.

Another night, two employees were at the General Wayne setting up the restaurant for a wedding on Saturday. When they left at 4 a.m., they were confident they had locked the door. When they returned a few hours later, at 9:30 a.m., the napkins were scattered across the floor. But only the napkins. The silverware, plates, and flowers were still set perfectly on each table.

One day Johnson decided to close the restaurant early due to a snowstorm. The chef, who had been cleaning, set a stack of hand-sized Turkish towels on the butcher block before everyone left. When they came back the next day, the towels had been thrown around the kitchen.

Johnson's wife was not exempt from the hauntings. She was working in the office totaling up the previous day's receipts when she noticed the adding machine was off. Repeatedly. Deciding that the machine must be broken, she asked Bart to go out and purchase a new one. While he was gone, she manually totaled up the numbers. She then checked her numbers with the new machine.

But the new machine didn't work, either. Even simple calculations like 2 + 2 came up wrong. Finally, she scolded the ghosts and told them she had work to do. As soon as she did, both machines worked correctly. After that, she learned to test the machine and if it didn't work right, she would order the ghosts out of the office.

Another ghostly prank was played on a patron who had refused to let the valets park his brand-new Cadillac. The customer was sitting in the restaurant with the car keys, when the car suddenly started up, headlights on, horn blaring and windshield wipers going. And this was before car keys had "panic" buttons and remote starts. One of the valets, who happened to be near the car at the time, ran inside to tell Johnson. "Calm down," Johnson told him. "These things happen around here. Just relax."

Dave Rogers would agree with Johnson. As he told author Michaeleen C. Maher, "Oh, you always heard banging on the walls, like creaking in the walls, lights flickering, the glasses shaking, wind—cold gusts of wind going past you real fast. It happened so often that we just—we eventually took it for granted. We just shrugged it off." Maher investigated the hauntings in 1988 for *Unsolved Mysteries*.

One thing that couldn't be shrugged off—or explained—was not as innocent. One morning, Johnson discovered the bar's cash drawer filled with water, ruining the machine. He called his insurance company to file a claim.

The insurance adjuster investigating the claim thought a leak in the roof caused the damage. He asked if he could go look at the roof. When he came back, he told Johnson, "I don't think your roof leaked."

"I don't think so either," Johnson replied. He had already come to that conclusion since it hadn't rained the night before.

"How did the water get in the drawer?" the adjuster asked.

"I don't know." Johnson wasn't sure if ghosts were covered by his insurance, but he wasn't about to learn.

As Johnson explained later, "[W]hat I didn't tell him, because he really wouldn't have believed me . . . was that in addition to the water being in the drawer of the cash register right to the brim, that across the other side of the bar there were thirty wine carafes . . . filled to the brim with water." Nor did Johnson mention the forty glasses above the register or the speed rack that had also been filled with water.

Soldiers are not the only ones who haunt here. Edgar Allan Poe's ghost has been seen sitting in his favorite corner of the inn on a few occasions. Poe was a frequent visitor to the inn between 1839 and 1843 and may have written a portion of "The Raven" here. A window in the inn had the letters EAP carved on it, which was believed to have been done by Poe during one of his visits. The window was broken either in the 1930s or the 1970s (stories differ) and no pictures of it exist.

People have also heard a child crying in the inn even though no children were there. During a séance in 1972, psychic Jean Quinn claimed to have made contact with a young boy who told her he had lost his mother. The child would not stop crying long enough to give her his name or any more information. An African-American man that Johnson believes is a former employee named Chase has also been seen. Chase had died shortly after Johnson purchased the inn.

A colonial woman or women haunt the second floor and the bar area. On the second floor, she motions people to be quiet. According to a psychic, she is afraid the noises will wake her baby. A colonial woman was also seen by author Beth Scott when she was interviewing Bart Johnson for her book *Historic Haunted America*. As she was sitting by the bar, "a distinct figure of a woman in a long, billowing white skirt and long-sleeved blouse hurried past the dark-paneled wall."

Most of the ghostly activity was reported when Bart Johnson owned the restaurant. Johnson owned it from 1970 until he decided to retire in November 1995. The General Wayne Inn was then sold to two best friends James "Jim" Webb and Guy Sileo.

According to author Laurie Hull, who met Webb during an investigation, the restaurant continued to have paranormal activity during their ownership. During her visit, she and her group witnessed one crystal on a chandler swinging back and forth while the other crystals were still. Webb told her that it happened quite frequently, but he didn't know what caused it.

DEATH AT THE INN

Tragically, on the night of December 26, 1996, Webb was found in the office shot in the back of the head. Police had several suspects but were unable to make any arrests in the case. The mystery around Webb's death intensified when, two months later, on February 22, 1997, twenty-year-old sous chef Felicia Moyse was also found shot in the head. On the night Jim had been shot, Moyse had been one of the last people to see him alive. She was also the alibi for the police's prime suspect: Jim's best friend and partner, Guy Sileo.

Sileo and Moyse had been having an affair at the time of Webb's murder. The two had since broken up and Sileo had gone back to his wife. Investigators decided that Moyse had been upset over the broken romance and committed suicide, although no suicide note was ever found.

Four months after Webb's death, the restaurant closed and Sileo filed for bankruptcy. He was later arrested and convicted for Webb's death. He had wanted to use the life insurance policy he had on Webb to pay off his debts. He tried to claim that Moyse had killed Webb because he didn't approve of her having an affair with a married man.

For the next ten years, the General Wayne Inn changed hands a number of times. But the restaurant that had become famous for murders committed on its site could not escape the taint of the more recent murder.

In 2005, the General Wayne Inn reopened as the Chabad Center for Jewish Life, a combination synagogue, kosher restaurant, and Chabad-Lubavitch outreach center. And while the outside may look the same, the inside has been massively renovated, which may have included relocating the ghosts. According to Rabbi Shraga Sherman in a May 10, 2004, *Philadelphia Inquirer* article, "The question people ask is: What about the ghosts in the building? Well, with a mezuzah on every door, whatever negativity transpired in this building, the positivity and holiness that we're going to bring in will marginalize it and push it out the door."

Laurie Hull visited the site a few years later while working on her book, *Philly's Main Line Haunts* and says that the ghosts seem to be lurking around the edges of the property, as if they are waiting for their opportunity to get back into the inn.

SIDE HAUNTS: WHY DOESN'T GENERAL WAYNE HAUNT THE GENERAL WAYNE INN?

With all the ghosts haunting the General Wayne Inn, you may be asking where the General himself is. Well, unfortunately his ghost is too busy trying to gather his lost bones to haunt the inn. He also happens to be one of the few people who are literally buried in two places at the same time.

Major General Anthony Wayne died on December 15, 1796, at Fort Presque Isle. The soldier, who had bravely fought the British and defeated the Indians, was done in by gout. Per Wayne's request, the soldiers dressed him in his best uniform and buried him by the camp's flagstaff.

After twelve years went by, Wayne's daughter, Margaretta, decided her father should be buried in the family plot, located in southeast Pennsylvania. She enlisted her brother, Isaac, to fetch the body. The siblings consulted with Dr. Benjamin Rush, who assured them that all that would be left would be bones that could be easily boxed up.

Isaac arrived in Erie in September 1809 and met with Dr. John C. Wallace, the same doctor who had been called but had arrived too late to help Major Wayne years before. But much to their dismay the body they uncovered was almost perfectly preserved. Only one leg had decayed.

Isaac now had a problem. Based on Dr. Rush's words, he had ridden to the fort in a sulky. His father's body would not fit in the two-wheeled carriage as it was. He didn't know what to do. He either had to return home and fetch a larger carriage or abandon his mission.

After much debate, Wallace suggested something he had learned from the Native Americans. If they dismembered the body and boiled it, the flesh would drop off. The now-cleaned bones could then be packed into boxes and fit into the sulky.

The two men accomplished the task. After it was done, Wallace tossed the flesh along with the instruments used to accomplish the task into the coffin and reburied it in the former grave. The gruesome task over, Isaac proceeded to take his father's bones home.

According to legend, something happened on the journey home and not all the bones completed the trip. Either the box tipped out of the carriage or the lid wasn't securely fastened, and the contents jostled out on the rough road.

No one knows why bones were lost on the journey home. But the loss of his bones has upset General Wayne. Every year on New Year's Day (his birthday) his spirit rises out of his new grave in Radnor and rides across the state of Pennsylvania on PA Road 322 to his original burial place, searching for his missing bones.

The original grave was lost in 1853 after the abandoned blockhouse burned down. In 1878, the gravesite was disturbed a second time and the coffin lid, clothing remnants, and instruments were recovered. The cauldron used is currently on exhibit at the Erie County Historical Society. Everything else was reburied in a reconstructed "Wayne's Blockhouse" monument on the grounds of the Pennsylvania Soldiers and Sailors Home.

Chapter 21
Universities

Approximately ninety colleges and universities reside in the greater Philadelphia area. While most of them probably claim a ghost or two, a few have more legendary tales, like that of Temple University Founder Dr. Conwell, who claimed to have been visited by his wife's ghost. Chestnut Hill has gone so far as to proclaim on their website that they are haunted, even if their faculty doesn't like to discuss it.

TEMPLE UNIVERSITY
2020 N. BROAD STREET

"I received three strange visits from my wife," Rev. Dr. Russell Conwell told the congregation of Grace Baptist Temple one Sunday. "On three successive nights she seemed to come and sit on the side of the bed which I occupied."

A wife sitting on her husband's bed wouldn't seem strange to most people, until they learned that Conwell's wife died five years before her visit. Conwell, the founder and then president of Temple University, claimed to have seen a ghost. He had been searching for his Civil War discharge papers, but neither he nor any of his staff could find them until Sarah appeared.

"While sitting there she gave me valuable information relating to several important papers which I knew were in the house, but I could not locate," Conwell explained. "It may have been a dream, but I got out of bed immediately after receiving the instructions and found the papers just where she said they were."

According to Conwell, "Three years after the death of my wife I began to see a form sitting on the side of my bed, at the foot, every morning when I woke." Conwell dismissed the visions as an "overwork on [his] eyesight" according to an article he wrote for *The Baptist*, a sectarian publication. But the vision of his wife grew stronger, unnerving Conwell enough that he consulted two physicians. They told him that the apparition would disappear if he reduced the hours he worked.

The doctor's advice made sense. Since Mrs. Conwell's passing, people noticed Dr. Conwell had become cold and distant. Perhaps grief caused the reverend to snap. His maid certainly thought he had cracked when he told her that Sarah's ghost helped him find his long-lost Civil War discharge papers. But that didn't explain how he managed to find them in a black-lacquered box hidden behind a bookcase in Conwell's library. They had been searching for weeks for them.

Conwell decided to prove Sarah's spirit was visiting him. He asked the maid to hide a gold pencil somewhere in the house where he would not find it. That night, Sarah sat on the bed and told him he would find it on the top shelf of the medicine cabinet, hidden toward the back. The following morning, Conwell returned the pencil to the astonished maid.

Conwell never claimed he had seen a ghost. In a December 18, 1919, article in the *New York Times* he said, "I have never been able to decide what it was, but I do know that I was unable to locate those papers until I received the messages from my wife." In the same article, Dr. Joseph Leidy, Jr., an "eminent physician" of New York City, attributed the ghostly visit to an unnamed psychological condition and to "unconscious cerebration" or unconscious thought.

Finding the pencil was the third and last time Sarah appeared fully to him. Urban legend says she was insulted by her husband's need to prove her existence to others, although Conwell claimed he still felt her presence around him. When he passed away, he was buried beside her in Monument Cemetery.

Ironically, in 1956 the final resting place of Conwell and his wife was disturbed by none other than Temple University. The University wanted to expand and purchased the cemetery. (For more information about Monument Cemetery see the Betsy Ross Bridge entry in chapter 2.) The Conwells were moved temporarily to Mount Laurel Cemetery until June 1959, when they were buried in the sidewalk alcove on North Broad Street between Conwell and Wachman Halls. In 1968, the couple was moved again to the newly constructed Founder's Garden, where they have remained.

Disturbing his resting place has caused Russell Conwell's ghost to haunt the main campus of Temple, but no one has gone on record claiming to see his ghost. He doesn't haunt Peabody Campus, where his home once stood, however. Gertrude Peabody does that haunting herself.

Peabody began teaching in 1923 as a home economics instructor. By 1930, she had risen to the position of Dean of Women. When Temple completed the new residence hall in 1958, they decided to dedicate it to Gertrude Peabody. Peabody left the University the following year—or did she?

Residents of Peabody Hall claim her ghost haunts the lobby and elevators of Peabody Hall. Some say she haunts the building because she committed suicide on the fourth floor of the building while she was still Dean of Students.

The story initially seems believable since she disappeared in 1959 after she was replaced as dean. Temple offers no biography on their website and only mentions that she was dean until 1959. Perhaps Temple decided to cover up her suicide. They don't like to discuss their scandals. After all, in their biography of Conwell they say "Conwell died December 6, 1925. [He and his wife, Sarah] were buried with full honors in a small courtyard next to Conwell Hall." They make no mention of his two previous burials, although they mention moving him in 1968.

Alas, Peabody went home to Maine, where she lived out her retirement until passing away on March 30, 1979.

PHILADELPHIA UNIVERSITY OF THE ARTS
320 SOUTH BROAD STREET

Philadelphia University of the Arts claims several ghosts haunt its campus. In Furness Hall, a student who hung himself haunts the building. People hear disembodied whispering and footsteps. Others report feeling inexplicably sad or that they are being watched. Even more disturbing are the people who are touched. One claimed an unseen force punched him in the stomach. A female reported she was smacked. She also claims that when she called security, they told her that they refuse to enter the building at night. Since few men will report being scared, even by ghosts, this excuse sounds a bit far-fetched.

Spruce Hall has a poltergeist that likes to make items disappear (only to return them months later) and mess with computers. A small dark-haired lady in a white dress has also been seen here. Most people say she gives off a feeling of sadness and loneliness.

The Merriam Theatre Building is haunted by a lady in white. She only appears when the building is empty or nearly empty. She is usually found toward the back of the theater in the highest seats or behind the stage. Ironically, one building that doesn't claim to be haunted, but has every reason to be, is the Juniper Residence Hall. This building was built over St. Mary's Cemetery.

CHESTNUT HILL COLLEGE
9601 GERMANTOWN AVENUE

According to Chestnut Hill College's website, they do not have a ghost haunting its grounds—they have several. The site proudly proclaims the college's paranormal activities have spanned decades and occur in several locations across their campus. And to give them credit, they do seem to have quite a few ghosts. So let's start the ghostly campus tour.

St. Joseph's Hall has several spirits. The first is a young nun who leaped from the Bishop's steps after giving birth to a priest's child. (The school used to be a convent.) She can be seen "floating" around the floor. A set of locked doors in the building keeps prying eyes away from a crucifix where the woman placed her child before her death. If you knock three times on the doors, you will get three raps in return. The art room is also said to be haunted by a former teacher. A ghost also haunts the basement, although this may be the ghost of the art teacher.

This is the same building where seventy-one-year-old adjunct professor Rudolf Alexandrov committed suicide in August 2011. He was about to start his class when he became upset and walked out. He then returned to his class, shouted something, and then ran to a ledge on the second floor. Two witnesses attempted to talk him out of it, but were unsuccessful. On April 16, 2014, a twenty-two-year-old male student was found dead on a couch in St. Joseph's Hall. The cause of death was never revealed.

The Logue Library is rumored to be built over a cemetery, which had already been moved twice. The construction disturbed the spirits that now haunt the library. Books and carts move on their own. The spirits are supposed to be more active after 11 p.m.

Fontbonne Hall, located next door to Logue Library and the Cemetery, is haunted by a young girl who died here during a flu epidemic. She wanders the third floor with an unknown male spirit. In one of the rooms, doors open and close on their own, electronic devices turn on and off, and both the shower and faucet will turn themselves on and off. Roommates are said to have the same dream of the woman on the same night. (Some accounts have placed this ghost and haunted room on the second floor of Fournier Hall.) Underneath the building is a tunnel that led to the Motherhouse (so called because it was once inhabited by nuns) where a crying woman has been heard.

A room on the second floor of Fournier Hall is called the "Red Eye Room" because two red eyes have been reported to float throughout the room. On the third floor, a young boy dressed in 1920s clothing has been seen. In the lower parking lot, between the sports field and the cemetery, the spirit of a young girl who was raped and murdered nearby appears to women walking alone.

Other ghosts supposed to haunt Chestnut Hill include a young lady with a beautiful brooch, a benevolent old man in robes, little girls who like to play dice games, and a boy with a "hair of fire and emerald eyes."

And although the college website admits the existence of the ghosts, the staff is a different matter. When asked about the ghostly occurrences, Kathleen Spigelmyer, Director of Communications at Chestnut Hill, said, "While I believe that these Chestnut Hill College myths . . . would make a fascinating read, there is no truth or supporting evidence to conclude that any of these events actually have happened on campus."

This statement contradicts the website, which said the "Campus Culture's dossier of the College's paranormal activity chronicles an extensive record spanning generations of curious, unexplained noises, doors seemingly locking and unlocking on their own, and several ghost sightings." Requests for clarification of the contradiction did not get a response.

PHILADELPHIA UNIVERSITY
4201 HENRY AVENUE

Ravenhill Mansion's gothic features make it the perfect background for a ghost story, which it kindly provides. The mansion had been given to the Archdiocese of Philadelphia in 1910 by Ann Marie Weightman, who had inherited it after her father died. The Archdiocese passed it to an order of nuns in 1919, Religious of the Assumption, who opened the private girls' school called Ravenhill Academy. Ravenhill became a prestigious school famous for its former student Grace Kelly. Today Ravenhill Mansion houses the administrative and faculty offices for Philadelphia University.

According to the legend, during the Mansion's Academy days, a nun became pregnant while having an affair with a priest. Ashamed and unable to acknowledge her misdeeds, she committed suicide in the attic.

If you sit on the hill located in front of the mansion at daybreak, you may catch sight of the nun walking around the property and in or near the attic where she died. Some also say the priest guilty in the affair has been sighted on the grounds.

Workers in the building have reported hearing noises. Fuzzy, glowing, white orbs appear in pictures. The attic lights turn themselves on, even though the door is always locked. But secrets won't always stay behind a locked door, as two former residents learned.

Nearby Fortress Hall also experiences poltergeist-like activity, although the identity of the ghost is unclear. Residents who wish to remain anonymous report a variety of events that have occurred without any known cause, including door handles rattling, toilets flushing, water dripping on them during their sleep, windows and closet doors opening and closing, and TV channels changing. Objects were also known to move about, such as one night when paper plates flew across the room. Orbs are also commonly photographed here.

SAINT JOSEPH'S UNIVERSITY
5600 CITY AVENUE

Saint Mary's Annex at Saint Joseph's University has several ghosts. Both residents and faculty have reported hearing footsteps, strange noises, and laughter in the building. Ghostly nuns are also seen walking the halls. The Annex was once a convent for the Sisters of Bon Secour before the University purchased it in the 1950s and converted into a residence hall. Saint Joseph's University is located in Merion

Station, and Saint Mary's Annex is located on McShain Driveway just off City Avenue.

UNIVERSITY OF PENNSYLVANIA MUSEUM OF ARCHAEOLOGY AND ANTHROPOLOGY
3260 SOUTH STREET

In December 2006, security cameras at the University of Pennsylvania Museum of Archaeology and Anthropology caught an image believed to be a ghost. According to Brian McDevitt, director of building operations, "It looked like a man who had a long trench coat, a scarf, and a hat." But more importantly, the image was "floating." The spirit was witnessed on several occasions over a two-month period in the Etruscan corridor. Since then, the museum frequently holds events that invite people to explore the museum's paranormal side and have a close encounter with a mummy.

UNIVERSITY OF THE SCIENCES
510 SOUTH FORTY-SECOND STREET

Legend says that University of the Sciences' Osol Hall was originally a psychiatric institute. During that time, a girl was mistreated and committed suicide on the sixth floor. Her spirit lifts toilet seats, makes "strange noises," and causes "strange sensations and weird feelings" for residents. However, the building was never a psychiatric institute, nor was there ever one at that location. Before it was transformed into a dorm, it was an office building.

Part Seven

SOUTH PHILLY

South Philadelphia has the unique distinction of being almost surrounded by water: the Schuylkill River on the west and the Delaware River on the east and south sides. Beyond that distinction, it consists of everything located south of South Street.

South Philadelphia is one of the largest Italian neighborhoods in the country and is where the "Italian Stallion" Rocky Balboa called home. South Philly is also home to the rival cheesesteak shops Geno's Steaks and Pat's King of Steaks.

But the most famous landmark here is the South Philadelphia Sports Complex. It is located at the corner of Broad Street and Pattinson Avenue and includes the Wells Fargo Center, Lincoln Financial Field, Citizens Bank Park, and Xfinity Live! which allows Philadelphia's professional baseball, football, ice hockey, basketball, lacrosse, and arena football teams to play in the same area.

Chapter 22
Fort
Mifflin

Fort Mifflin gets most people's vote as "most haunted place in Philadelphia" due to the number of ghosts reported and the length of time it has been haunted. The first story dates back to 1778 when wailing women were heard mourning the men who died during the siege. Thankfully, this historic site has learned to embrace its ghosts with pride.

FORT MIFFLIN
82 FORT MIFFLIN ROAD

Office manager Lorraine Irby was asleep when she was woken up. "All of a sudden I heard a god-awful, terrible scream; I really thought that one of our visitors was hurt. It was a very disturbing scream like someone was being tortured and murdered," says Irby.

Fearing that something had happened to one of the ghost-hunting guests that were spending the night, she ran out to investigate. She found two people sitting on the porch of the Officer's Quarters. They did not seem troubled.

"Did you hear that scream?" Irby asked. Both shook their heads no. It was then Irby realized she must have heard the Screaming Woman, one of the most famous ghosts at Fort Mifflin.

Fort Mifflin was commissioned in 1771. It sits on Mud Island (also known as Deep Water Island) on the Delaware River south of the Schuylkill River and Philadelphia. American forces secured the fort in 1775, although it wasn't until two years later that the location would see real action.

After the British took control of Philadelphia, they set their sights on the fort. For six weeks, approximately 450 Americans were able to keep the British at bay during a battle now known as the Siege of Fort Mifflin.

The siege ended on November 15, when the British sailed several ships up to Fort Mifflin carrying over 200 cannons and launched a naval assault on the fort. All afternoon the British attacked. In one hour, one thousand cannonballs were fired at the fort. Out-gunned, the Americans were forced to retreat, but not before more than half the men had been killed or wounded. The Americans' last action was to set fire to the fort as they left.

Fort Mifflin laid in ruins until around 1795, when the fort was reconstructed in an effort to rebuild American defenses. During the Civil War, the fort was used to house prisoners, including Confederates captured during the Battle of Gettysburg. By 1864, 216 Confederate soldiers, 55 Union soldiers, and 11 civilians were held here to await trial or sentencing.

The sound of a woman screaming within the walls of Fort Mifflin has been heard on numerous occasions by various people, both employees and visitors. It is also one of the oldest reported hauntings. Urban legend says that the sound of women wailing was heard as far back as 1778. They were believed to be women mourning the loss of the men killed during the siege of Fort Mifflin.

On several occasions, the screaming at night has been so loud that the Philadelphia police have been summoned. The screaming is often believed to be coming from the second floor of the officers' quarters.

Many of the stories about the ghost identify her as Elizabeth Pratt. According to legend, Pratt was either married to a sergeant stationed at Fort Mifflin or lived near the fort in the early 1800s. While here, her daughter fell in love with a soldier. For some reason, Elizabeth didn't approve and disowned her daughter. The daughter died soon after (either from dysentery or typhoid fever). Consumed with guilt, Pratt committed suicide by hanging herself over the second-floor balcony of the officers' quarters.

Tony Selletti claims in his 2008 book *Fort Mifflin: A Paranormal History* that Elizabeth Pratt never lived in the officers' quarters but was housed in a building that once sat where the artillery shed is now. According to his research in the archives at the fort, Pratt lost two young children in 1802 and died in 1803. Her cause of death is not listed, but she couldn't have committed suicide in the officers' quarters since the building wasn't completed until 1814.

Some have also offered another identity of the screaming woman: Elizabeth Bunker. Her husband was stationed at Fort Mifflin in 1863 when she died of gastritis. However, no explanation has been given to explain why Bunker might be screaming at the fort or why the screaming woman's name must be Elizabeth.

Another possibility exists for the sounds of screaming at the fort. A number of animals make noises that sound like a woman screaming when mating or in distress, including owls (especially screech and barn), red-tailed hawks, red foxes, eagles, goats, possums, raccoons, and domestic cats, all of which are native to the Philadelphia area. Mountain lions, fisher cats, and bobcats could also have been the cause in the past, although they are no longer found in Eastern Pennsylvania. If this sounds far-fetched, consider that on two separate occasions in 2013—once in England and the other in Australia—police were called out to investigate a report of woman screaming. In both cases, the offender turned out to be a red fox.

But animals can't explain the numerous sightings of a woman inside the officer's quarters. On one occasion after being called to investigate the sound of screaming, rumors say the police chased the figure of a female across the ramparts until she disappeared before their eyes.

More credible are children who claim to see a woman standing in the window of the second floor of the officers' quarters. Staff at Fort Mifflin purposefully avoid talking about the ghosts with children, since they don't want them to be afraid of the historical site.

On one occasion, a guide was giving a tour to a group of schoolchildren when the children's faces turned ashen and some began crying. "Who is the woman in the window?" they asked. "What is wrong with her?" The guide turned to look where they were pointing but didn't see anything in the window.

Sadly, on March 23, 2014, an electrical fire broke out on the second floor of the building. A caretaker sleeping there was able to get out safely, but the structure and historical items were damaged. Ironically, it was the second fire at Fort Mifflin during a Boy Scout overnight camping experience. The first one, on October 26, 1980, happened when Boy Scouts entered the Commandant's House seeking shelter from the rain and then decided to start a fire, which destroyed everything but the exterior of the building. In a twist of fate, during the more recent outing, one of the chaperones for the Scouts happened to be a firefighter and was able to contain the fire using extinguishers until help arrived.

While every inch of the fort appears to be haunted, some of the most chilling tales come from the casemates. Casemates are small rooms in the walls of the fortress from which guns can be fired. Although the rooms were never used for this purpose at Fort Mifflin, soldiers found other uses for them. Through the years they have been used for storage, as a chapel, as barracks, and as a prison—the latter is why they are often referred to as "the dungeon." During the Civil War, more than 200 Union and Confederate soldiers were kept within the casemates.

One of the ghosts frequently seen in Casemate 5, as well as other locations in Fort Mifflin, is the "Faceless Man." Typically people see a man sitting in the casement sewing with a "black hole" where his face should be. On two separate occasions people have caught an image of a tall man—more than six feet high—wearing a "sloppy coat" but no face. Some people have described the faceless man as "mocking" and "mean."

He may also be the same ghost that haunts Casemate 4. Here visitors have been pinched, grabbed, and experienced an "unpleasant sensation." Blonde women are a favorite target. They have had their hair pulled and have even reported feeling as if someone was trying to strangle them.

Many say that the ghost in Casemate 4 and 5 is that of William "Billy" Howe, who was executed at the fort on August 26, 1865. According to the story, authorities sold tickets to the hanging, which turned it into a party. Howe was particularly upset with the giggling women in the crowd and is seeking revenge against them from the grave.

While the story sounds heart-wrenching, it doesn't match the historical record. Howe fought in the Civil War at the Battle of Fredericksburg. He was one of only five men who came off the field of carnage with the colors of his regiment. According to an August 27, 1865, article in the *Philadelphia Inquirer*, after his regiment left the field, Howe exchanged his musket for an Enfield rifle and went back to the field. He remained there overnight and into the following day, when he barely escaped being captured by the enemy.

After the battle, Howe contracted "Inflammation of the Bowels" and was ordered to Washington for medical treatment because the regimental hospital had burned down. When neither he nor his friend Agustus Beiting could find treatment there, they decided to return to their homes to recover.

For the next two months, Howe remained bedridden. Then one rainy night, Abraham Bartolet and three other men came to his house to arrest Howe for desertion. When Howe's wife refused to open the door, the men began hammering on it to gain entrance. Howe fired two shots out the window. Whether he knew why the men were there has never been clearly established, but it does not appear that he intended to kill anyone. Unfortunately, one of the bullets struck and killed Bartolet.

Howe was arrested several days later and brought to Fort Mifflin to stand trial for desertion and murder. He was found guilty of both charges and sentenced to death. While awaiting sentencing, Howe attempted to escape, which caused authorities to transfer him to Eastern State Penitentiary. It was there he bid a farewell to his wife and sons in a scene so heartbreaking that "even the jailor, who is accustomed to such sights, acknowledged it was one of the most heart-rending scenes he had ever witnessed."

Before his execution, Howe asked for forgiveness from anyone he had harmed and even thanked the Judge Advocate and his lawyer for showing him kindness. The *Inquirer* article also described Howe as a man "about five feet eight inches in height" and having a "mild disposition." In other words, not tall or mean as people describe the Faceless Man.

Other possibilities exist for the ghost, however. Approximately thirty prisoners died here during the Civil War. Any one (or more) could be causing the haunting, as seems to be the case in the other casemates.

In Casemate 1, a soldier dressed in Revolutionary War apparel has been spotted standing near the fireplace. During one investigation, an EVP captured a voice identifying himself as "Michael." People have also reported seeing one of the bunks moving by itself.

On the other side of the fort is Casemate 11. It wasn't discovered until 2006, but it didn't take long for ghosts to move in. The ghosts here do not seem to like visitors since EVP sessions have recorded a voice telling them to "get out." People also report feeling uneasy here.

Interestingly, the name "W. H. Howe" was found carved into the wall of Casemate 11. Howe was probably kept here after his escape attempt before being moved to Eastern State. One important footnote in the Howe case occurred a year to the day after his death. On August 26, 1865, President Andrew Johnson ordered Howe's sentence commuted from death to imprisonment and a dishonorable discharge. Not really exoneration, but I suppose you take what you can get. (Someone should have told Johnson that you can't reverse a death sentence after it has been carried out.)

In the blacksmith shop, a spirit likes to open and close the doors, swing tools hanging on the wall, and move objects around. The sound of a hammer clanging against an anvil is also heard coming from the empty shop. Employees and visitors have also seen a shadowy figure walking near the front of the shop.

The ghost is said to be Jacob Sauer, who argued with the Commandant about keeping the shop's backdoor open, which was not allowed. It seemed Sauer was determined to win the argument, even if it was beyond the grave. Staff would constantly find the door open, even if they had locked it. The constant opening and closing caused the hinges to deteriorate until Jacob got his way: the door was permanently removed. No historical evidence has supported this claim or the identity of the ghost, however.

"The Lamplighter" is a ghost seen carrying around an oil-burning lamp and lighting lanterns that no longer exist. He doesn't seem to realize that the fort has electricity and his work is unnecessary. He is most commonly seen on the porticoes of the soldiers' barracks. According to Executive Director Dori McMunn, "We always thought it was a joke until we ran into documentation that we did indeed have oil lamps needed to be lit at twilight." A psychic identified him as "Joseph Adkins," but no evidence has been found to support this.

The powder magazine also has frequent paranormal incidents. Witnesses have reported seeing a soldier sitting in the far corner of the room. A man wearing a Revolutionary War uniform has been seen standing outside the door as if standing guard. A strange mist and shadowy figures are seen walking about, usually moving from the building up the embankment. Footsteps have been heard and even recorded walking in the hallway. Most people report feeling a negative presence watching them.

As previously explained, the Commandant's House was destroyed by a fire in 1980. But that hasn't caused the ghost to move out. Bells are heard coming from the building, although the bell tower is gone. Weeping has also been heard. More recently people report feeling someone or something touch them on their legs or feet.

One helpful ghost is the "tour guide." Visitors at Fort Mifflin mistake him for a tour guide dressed in Civil War period clothing. The guide takes them through the fort, giving them elaborate details. "It was as if he lived there," they would later proclaim when praising him to perplexed staff—perplexed, because they have no idea about whom the visitors are talking. Not only does his description not match any of their employees, but he shows up on days when no one is dressed in Civil War apparel.

As stated earlier, ghost sightings have been reported throughout the fort. A few of the more widely spread stories include:

- People report hearing children's voices and dogs barking, although neither is on the grounds.
- The disembodied voices of soldiers and sailors are heard. One tourist even recorded the sound of German being spoken near outer or water casements where Hessian soldiers attacked the fort during the Revolutionary War.
- An old-fashioned ship was seen docked by the fort.
- A "Sad-Looking Man" walks alone down the road to the gate of the fort before disappearing.

- The sound of a little girl calling for help or "Mommy" is heard near the Artillery Shed. She is believed to be a victim of the typhoid epidemic in the early eighteenth century. (This is where the officer's housing stood when Elizabeth Pratt lived at the fort.)
- Heavy footsteps have been heard on the second floor of the soldiers' quarters.
- People report feeling physically affected due to the "heavy feel" near the Southwest Sally Port. It makes them so uneasy that they are unable to stay for long.
- The feeling of being touched or poked is also experienced near the Southwest Sally Port.
- The smell of a wood fire or of baking bread has been reported.
- Electronic devices like cameras and recorders refuse to work properly or have batteries suddenly die, even after being replaced.

One of the most interesting and indisputable events occurred in 1997. Professional photographer Ray Morgenweck was photographing Civil War re-enactors at the fort using the original processes and equipment of the 1860s. According to Morgenweck, "When I developed the plate, I thought at first that the small markings to the upper right center were blemishes on the plate's surface. But on closer inspection, it appears to be a human who isn't exactly standing on the ground. What is it? I don't know."

Chapter 23

Ships

Penn's Landing is a ten-block strip of waterfront area along the Delaware River where one can find not one, but two haunted ships. Although the ships look like they are from different eras, both were launched at the turn of the nineteenth century and both served the United States during wartime.

USS *OLYMPIA*
PENN'S LANDING

As a merchant marine captain, Harry Burkhardt has had several experiences onboard ships, but nothing compares with what happened while working on the USS *Olympia*. It was Labor Day weekend and Burkhart was working in Boiler Room #5.

"I felt two hands grab my arms—and they were icy cold," he said. He turned around but found no one there. Shocked, he heard a female's voice say, "I think he's okay," followed by the sound of female laughter, but no one else was in the boiler room with him (that he could see). Burkhardt still can't explain what he experienced, but it was definitely strange.

Melissa Miller, founder and investigator with Ghost Research and Investigation of Pennsylvania (GRIP), was visiting the ship's boiler room when she felt someone was with her. She turned on her recorder and asked if someone was there. When she listened to the recording, she heard a man saying, "I think I'm in love."

People in the boiler room have heard footsteps walking overhead, although the floor above them is two inches thick. Shadow figures have also been witnessed walking from the passage into the boiler room and from the boiler room to the coal room.

The USS *Olympia* was launched on November 5, 1892, and commissioned on February 5, 1895. On May 1, 1898, Navy Commodore George Dewey stood on her bridge and said his famous line, "You may fire when you are ready, Gridley." Gridley complied and fired the opening shots of the Battle of Manila Bay, the first battle in the Spanish-American War. The Olympia is the last surviving warship from that war and the oldest steel warship still afloat in the world.

During World War I, she transported the remains of the Unknown Soldier from France. She was decommissioned in December 1922 and placed in reserve. On September 11, 1957, she became a maritime museum. She is permanently moored at Penn's Landing next to the USS *Becuna* and the *Moshulu*.

One of the first deaths on board the *Olympia* happened on April 24, 1895. During a firing exercise, Coxswain John Johnson was set to fire Portside #2 gun when it broke loose from the gun carriage and smashed him into the side of the ship. Johnson died instantly.

The event was memorialized in a poem by a fellow crew member:

No chance for a prayer,
Not a word of farewell,
To his shipmates around
That loved him so well . . .
His frame, crushed and quivering,
Was borne to the deck;
"No hope," said our surgeon,
"It has broken his neck."

Johnson was buried with full military honors in a San Diego cemetery. Ever since his death, people have reported hearing knocking around the area where he died. Connie Burkhardt was a volunteer on the ship when she heard it.

According to Connie, "I was on the starboard side on the second deck near the galley. Something was knocking on the door right next to me. The door the knocking came from was actually a closet. It was a storage closet, padlocked shut. Someone was trying to get my attention."

Johnson's death cast a dark shadow over the ship and convinced many of its crew that it was somehow cursed. Shortly after Johnson's death, one of the ship's anchor chains gave way and almost severed an ensign's leg. Boiler fumes nearly overcame a cleaning crew. Several crew members were lost when the Pacific Mail steamer carrying them home to the East Coast sank in a typhoon.

Besides Johnson, eighteen other crew members have died on the *Olympia*. Not as the result of war, but due to accidents. For example, one crew member died when he fell forty feet from the deck into the engine room. Perhaps his spirit haunts the Starboard Engine Room.

In 2008, Harry Burkhardt's son, Kevin, was working in the engine room with another volunteer when they saw a dark figure dart across the doorway. Later that day, the two also saw a figure reflected in a pane of Plexiglas in another part of the ship. But when they turned around to see who had joined them, no one was there.

In July 2010, Melissa Miller saw a full-body apparition appear in front of her. "It came out of a corridor, turned right, walked [toward the back of the ship], and dissipated into the darkness," she explained. "I could see what he was wearing: boots, slacks, a button-down shirt, and short-brimmed hat."

Other people have also reported seeing shadows moving around the engine room and heard voices there. One such person is John Laurino, Historic Ships Assistant Manager at Independence Seaport Museum. He was in the room alone when he heard a voice. According to John, he "jumped about a foot in the air" when it startled him.

Although the engine and boiler rooms are said to be the most haunted parts of the ship, other parts of the ship are also reportedly haunted. In September 2010, several guests informed worker Chris Hall that they had seen a "translucent form of a man" appear in front of him. A man wearing a suit has been seen in the corridor at the rear of the ship.

Another man wearing a white navy uniform has been observed walking around the ship before vanishing. In August 2010, a person near the ship saw a man holding onto the ship's wheel. He turned back to get a better look, but the spirit was gone. On another occasion, an eight-year-old girl told her mother that she had seen a man standing inside one of the locked officer's staterooms vanish before her eyes.

Harry Burkhardt had another encounter while doing an EVP session. "We were sitting here in the crew's berth deck [in June] and asked, 'Do you mind us being here?' I got a flat-out, 'Get out!'" Burkhardt said. "You don't hear it at the time. You find it later when you play back the recording." He also picked up a voice saying, "Save the ship!"

But USS *Olympia*'s ghosts were not be enough to save her. As of November 2014, she was in danger of sinking into the Delaware River. Her steel hull needed to be replaced, which would cost approximately $7 million, and another $3 million was needed to replace her wood deck. And that is just the start of the possible renovation costs.

THE *MOSHULU*
PENN'S LANDING

Anyone who drives on I-95 between the Walt Whitman and Ben Franklin bridges notices the *Moshulu*. The 394-foot barque—a sailing vessel with three or more masts—is a landmark on Penn's Landing. Although her masts no longer hold the thirty-four sails used to take her around Cape Horn fifty-four times during her days at sea, she still strikes a spectacular picture on the Delaware River. And she has a remarkable history.

The *Moshulu* was launched from Port Glasgow, Scotland, in 1904 under the name *Kurt*. For its first ten years it transported supplies to a copper mine in Santa Rosalia, Mexico. In 1914, the *Kurt* voyaged to Astoria, Oregon, to pick up a grain cargo. It was still in port when World War I began. Its owners decided to keep the ship in port and out of the war. It didn't work. In 1917, the United States confiscated the ship and placed it in service to make voyages from the United States to Australia and the Philippines. The ship was renamed the *Dreadnaught*, after the famous clipper ship. But before it could sail under that name, First Lady Wilson renamed the ship the *Moshulu*, a Seneca word that means "one who fears nothing."

The government operated the ship until it was purchased by Charles Nelson Company in 1921. The ship hauled lumber along the West Coast along with voyages to Australia and South Africa until 1928. In 1934, Gustave Ericson purchased the *Moshulu*. Ericson had the largest fleet of square riggers in continuous operation. The ship was put back in service in the grain trade between Australia and Europe.

In 1939, owners of the square riggers held an informal race among the grain carriers to determine who could make the quickest journey from Australia to Europe around Cape Horn. The *Moshulu* won, but it was the last race as World War II broke out. In 1940, the Germans confiscated her. They stripped her of her masts and spars and used her as a floating warehouse. She continued in this capacity for various owners after the war ended.

She was headed to the scrapyard when she was purchased in 1970 by Raymond E. Wallace for Specialty Restaurants and brought to the United States to be converted to a boat restaurant. In 1975, The *Moshulu* opened as a boat restaurant on Penn's Landing.

In July 11, 1989, at 11 p.m. a four-alarm fire broke out on the ship while 200 people were on board. Patrons on the upper decks used ropes from the ship's rigging to swing to safety. No one was seriously injured and the fire was not hot enough to ruin the steel hull, but it gutted the interior. She was moved across the Delaware to the Broadway Terminal in Camden, New Jersey. It seemed that the ship was again destined to be scrapped until she was purchased by HMS Ventures, Inc. in 1994. Two years later, the *Moshulu* reopened after six million dollars' worth (although some reports say $11 million) of renovations were done. On July 24, 1996, Philadelphia Mayor Ed Rendell re-christened the *Moshulu* and she opened on Pier 34.

In May 2000, the *Moshulu* closed again after the dock beside her collapsed, killing three people. In 2002 she moved back to Penn's Landing next to the (also haunted) USS *Olympia* and reopened. Since then, she has won several awards for her exceptional and romantic dining.

Captain P. A. McDonald was in charge of the *Moshulu* in 1934 when she was purchased by Ericson. In a July 24, 1953, article he said, "Don't you believe old sailing ships have ghosts? Of course, they do! It's usually the carpenter or sailmaker [sic] who put much of themselves in to the vessels they sailed in. They rarely changed from ship to ship as did the other sailors and often died aboard a favorite vessel. Naturally they'd want to come back—occasionally, if not for keeps."

McDonald might have been referring to the *Moshulu* and one of her three ghosts. Her most famous ghost is known as the Lantern Ghost. On the dining tables in the restaurant sit fifty-two lanterns, each with its own candle. Before opening, these candles are all lit. After closing, the staff takes extreme care to extinguish them, especially after the 1989 fire (although it was caused by electrical work). But when they arrive in the morning, they are surprised to find the candles relit. Sometimes the ghost doesn't wait for the staff to leave. A worker will blow out a candle then move to the next table. After extinguishing that one, he finds the previous one has relit itself. According to general manager Eli Kareteny, almost every server has experienced this ghost.

A whispering ghost is heard on the top deck. Usually around early evening, staff and guests report hearing what is described as a man whispering down from the riggings. The voice is never loud enough for them to make out what is said. No one knows who the ghost is, but it could be one of the twenty-eight people who died during the *Moshulu*'s days at sea.

The final ghost is that of a woman heard laughing in the ladies room. When the staff is cleaning up after dinner service, they report hearing hysterical laughing. Thinking a guest is still in the restaurant, they investigate, only to find it empty.

How could a woman's ghost be found on the *Moshulu*? Some speculate she was the wife of one of her captains. She might also have been a woman who disguised herself as a man to get work on the ship. (Although if the former was true, wouldn't she enter the men's bathroom?)

If you get a sense of déjà vu when visiting this ship, don't be shocked. She was the ship seen in *The Godfather: Part II* when Vito Corleone arrives in America and in *Rocky* during one of Rocky's waterfront workout sessions.

Chapter 24

USS
Forrestal

The USS Forrestal *had a tragic history that created several ghosts during her history at sea. Even the Navy was forced to admit she was haunted given all the recorded events. Although some still may not believe, her record speaks for itself.*

USS *FORRESTAL*
(FORMERLY) NAVY YARD

Our military forces willingly enlist, knowing they may one day be asked to face death to defend their country. But no one told them "facing death" would mean dealing with the ghostly form of George, the nickname given to the ghost on the USS *Forrestal*—if they had, some of them might have thought twice about signing up.

When the USS *Forrestal* was commissioned in September 1955 she was the longest warship in the world, at 1,046 feet. Her construction cost $217 million. An estimated forty thousand people could stand on her super deck, although she only had a crew of four thousand. When she was sent to Vietnam in 1967, she was still the third-largest warship afloat.

Her first mission brought her to the Gulf of Tonkin. On July 29, 1967, at 10:51 a.m., the *Forrestal* was launching its fifth day of attacks when tragedy struck. Although the exact chain of events has never been uncovered, a camera on the deck recorded that a Zuni missile fired accidentally. The rocket hissed across the flight deck and through the auxiliary fuel tank of an A-4 Skyhawk. Inside the plane was Lt. Cmdr. Fred White. Fuel spilled out onto the deck between his plane and a Skyhawk where thirty-year-old Lt. Cmdr. John McCain was doing his preflight checks. White and McCain scrambled out of their planes to safety. Ninety seconds later at least one of the 1,000-pound AN-M65 bombs on their planes cooked off—exploded prematurely due to the surrounding heat—killing White and most of the ship's first wave of firefighters.

Within five minutes, nine major explosions rocked the ship. Black smoke billowed out from the fire as new explosions sent flaming debris in every direction. Within the hour, eight more bombs exploded. At one point, half of the ship was on fire. By the time the fire was extinguished eighteen hours later, 134 service members were dead and 161 were seriously injured (some reports put the number at 300 injured). It was the worst loss of life on a U.S. Navy ship since World War II. The *Forrestal* was sent back to Norfolk, Virginia, for repairs, but it never returned to Vietnam.

(John McCain survived the fire and transferred to the USS *Oriskany*, only to be shot down three months later over North Vietnam. He remained a prisoner of war until 1973. Despite years of torture that left him with permanent physical limitations, he was able to get his flight status reinstated in 1974 and continued serving in the military until he retired in 1981. The following year he entered the political arena, spending most of it as a U.S. Senator.)

The USS *Forrestal*'s ghost, George, became a public figure in July 1988 when the ship's public affairs officer, Lt. James Brooks, issued a twelve-page news release documenting George's activities. The report included a photograph of a disembodied pair of khaki slacks entering a hatch. At the time the picture was taken, the ship was patrolling the North Arabian Sea.

This was not the only sighting. Mess Specialist 2nd Class Gary Weiss saw a man dressed in a khaki uniform climb down the ladder into pump room No. 1. But when Weiss checked the room, it was empty although the ladder is the only access. Petty Officer James Hillard had a similar experience when he saw a khaki-clad figure enter one of the compartments. But again, there was no one in there and no other way out.

On another occasion, Hillard was moving supplies when he heard a telephone ringing. According to Hillard, "The phone rang and I answered it. This time there was a faint voice calling, 'Help! Help! I'm on the sixth deck!'"

Hillard went to the sixth deck to check things out, but everything was fine. He might have believed that one of his friends was pulling a prank on him, until he noticed that the phone was out of service. "Rumor had it that a crew member was killed down there. I'm very scared to go down there alone," said Hillard after the experience. "If I do, I get out of there as fast as I can."

Petty Officer Daniel Balboa, who claimed not to believe the ship was haunted in the 1988 report, admitted he had some strange experiences in the ship.

"I was taking inventory one night and heard a noise like deck grating being picked up and dropped. I'd turn around and look but didn't see anything. When I turned around to begin my work again, the noise started again."

Another time, Balboa was in the food-storage freezer when he noticed the door open behind him. He closed the door, only to find it had opened again. "It is impossible for anyone to open the [refrigerator] doors from the outside, behind me," Balboa explained. "To open them from the outside requires a key since the doors lock automatically. I had the only key with me." After that, Balboa admitted he was close to believing in George's existence.

Weiss also had an experience with George inside the freezer. He and another crew member were inside the freezer when they heard a voice say, "Hello, shipmates!" Since they had the door shut, which makes the freezer soundproof, the noise had to have come from inside the freezer. Another crew member was in the same freezer looking for a box of hamburgers when he heard a thud behind him. Lying in the middle of the freezer was the exact box he was looking for. He couldn't have overlooked it because had it been there a moment earlier, he would have had to step over it.

Speculation about George's identity has led to several theories. He was given his nickname after a former food officer on the ship. After Brooks's press release, a Navy widow from Alabama wrote to him, suggesting it could be the ghost of her husband "Hank" who had been buried at sea off the *Forrestal* in April of that year. Since George's activities were recorded long before 1988, this seems unlikely. Another theory is that he is a pilot who died in 1986. The pilot did not die on the ship, but his body was stored in the morgue where George likes to haunt. Others say that he was a chief petty officer killed in the 1967 fire.

More likely, "George" is not one ghost, but several ghosts haunting the ship. This could explain why a pilot stationed on the ship in 1992 reported seeing a man dressed in an old-fashioned Naval uniform of a blue chambray shirt, dark blue trousers, and a white sailor hat on the port quarter of the fantail. The pilot claimed the man was there one second and gone the next.

Reports of George opening locked doors, turning lights on and off, and walking up and down the lower levels are fairly common. But some events have been more sinister. According to Petty Officer 3rd Class Jeff McElhannon, "People have been pushed, things thrown around, people woken up for no apparent reason."

Another man reported feeling a hand grab his ankle as he climbed the stairs near the freezer. But when he looked down, the room was empty. He was lucky. Another sailor was climbing a ladder when something grabbed him around the legs. The hold was so tight that one of his shipmates had to pull him free.

Air crewman Tim Madrid was stationed on the ship in 1982 when he reported that he heard "voices in the night crying for help" and saw a sailor "walk into an area that was just a plain old bulkhead. He would completely disappear."

During her service, the ship was known informally as the "USS Zippo," the "Forest Fire," and "Firestal." This was not an insensitive way of referring to the 1969 tragedy but because of a number of other fires aboard the ship, including:

- Two days before the July 29, 1967, fire, two separate fires erupted onboard ship. Both fires were extinguished within minutes.

- On July 31, 1967, while moored at Subic Bay, fire broke out in a pile of still smoldering mattresses. Witnesses noted the crew seemed slower to respond. As one officer on the pier noted, "They're probably immune to it by now."

- July 13, 1969, while still in dry dock at Norfolk Naval Shipyard, a load with two thousand aircraft wheels caught fire. Eight crew members were injured.

- On July 10, 1972, while the ship was at the Naval Base in Norfolk, a fire caused heavy damages and destroyed computers. Repairs took three months and cost $7.5 million. Seaman Apprentice Jeffrey Allison was convicted of arson for the blaze.

- On January 13, 1978, an A-7E Corsair II from VA-81 crashed on the flight deck. Two deck crew members were killed and eight others were injured. It crashed into two parked planes and then skidded across the deck in flames. Fuel spilled onto the aft portion of the deck and caused a small fire.

- On May 21, 1978, boxes caught fire in a storeroom, spreading smoke throughout the third deck. The fire was put out within ten minutes.

- On April 8, 1978, a fire erupted in Number Three Main Machinery Room. Hot steam lines had set fire to freshly painted lagging.

- On April 11, 1978, a fire was discovered in a catapult steam trunk and in an adjoining storeroom. Both fires were out within an hour.

- In June 26, 1979, while at Mayport Naval Station in Florida, three minor fires occurred on board. Again the cause was arson.

- On October 9, 1989, an electrical fire in the forward elevator machinery room injured nine crew members. The fire delayed the ship's twentieth major deployment.

Although the fires have never been attributed to ghosts, the danger may have encouraged at least one spirit to stay on the ship. According to Byron "Barney" Haslam, he and another sailor had accidentally fallen asleep while working the night shift in the boiler room. Suddenly he was woken up by someone shaking him and saying, "Hey!" But his coworker was still asleep and no one else was in the room.

He went to check the boilers and discovered that bad fuel had extinguished the fire inside one of the boilers. According to Haslam, "We were 50 gallons of water away from being vaporized when raw fuel would have lit off the back wall of the affected boiler. I don't know if it was a *Forrestal* ghost or my guardian angel, but someone saved my life."

The *Forrestal* continued to be deployed until September 11, 1993, when she was decommissioned at Pier 6E in Philadelphia. Sightings of "George" continued. In 1993, while the ship was moored in the Philadelphia Navy Yard, welder Stan Shimborski was dismantling the food storage equipment when he heard clanging. Thinking another worker had come on board and was banging hello, Shimborski used his wrench and clanged back. His reply was answered by more clanging.

Curious as to who it was (and why he kept banging on the walls), he decided to investigate. When he reached the other side of the compartment he saw "a chief petty officer horribly burned just staring at me. And then he slowly fades away."

The Navy offered the *Forrestal* as a possible museum, but nothing panned out. She spent several years moored in Newport, Rhode Island, before returning to Philadelphia in June 2010. She would remain in Philadelphia until February 2014 when she was towed to Brownsville, Texas, to be scrapped.

Author's note: While researching the events of July 29, 1967, I discovered several discrepancies on what occurred after the Zuni missile launched. Some of it was accusatory toward members of the *Forrestal* crew, suggesting that they were at fault or not as heroic as they could have been. Others have suggested that crew members did not react to the events as they have later claimed. I tried to include only the information that seems to be agreed upon by all involved. Everyone on board the ship that day is a hero in my eyes, as is everyone else who has served or is currently serving in the U.S. military.

SIDE HAUNTS: QUARTERS A, NAVY YARD
1413 LANGLEY AVENUE

Although the *Forrestal* is gone, ghosts still haunt the Navy Yard. People continue to report seeing ghostly figures of two men, sometimes with a black dog, walking around Quarters A of the Navy Yard. The ghosts have been described as both glowing and shadowy. Built in 1874 as a residence for the civil engineer in charge of construction of the Navy Yard,

Quarters A was later used as VIP quarters for visiting dignitaries and then as an officer's club. Today the building is used as office space for a technology company.

Part Eight

HAUNTED BURIAL GROUNDS

Philadelphia has a lot of cemeteries, although not as many as they once did. And the cemeteries tell a lot about Philadelphia's history, whether it be in the majesty of Laurel Hill, the oldest rural cemetery in Philadelphia, or the neglect of Mount Moriah (although some are trying to change that).

Philadelphia's cemeteries also tell the story of how the city has changed. Cemeteries once built on the edge of town were slowly enveloped as the city expanded. To make room for houses and other buildings, Philadelphia passed laws that enabled people to move cemeteries. And move them they did. A lot. Or at least that what people were told.

Chapter 25

Haunted Cemeteries

Ghosts love cemeteries. At least, that's what we grow up believing. Whether that's true or not, not many people are brave enough to walk through a cemetery alone at night. A city as old as Philadelphia, with some of the oldest cemeteries, is required by ghostly law to have a few haunted cemeteries.

Cemeteries have reputations for being haunted. An old superstition says that the spirit of the last person buried in a cemetery would forever stand watch over the cemetery. Another superstition required people passing by or through a cemetery to hold their breath to prevent breathing in the soul of a deceased person. Pallbearers wore gloves to prevent the soul of the deceased from passing through the coffin and into their bodies. (Although, if the soul can pass through the wood of the coffin, what prevents it from going through cloth?) English Saxons cut off the feet of their deceased to prevent the corpse from rising. (A tradition which fans of *The Walking Dead* are considering reviving, pardon the pun.)

Even without superstitions to warn us away, something about the thought of thousands of dead bodies lying two meters below your feet creeps people out. The high concentration of bodies within a cemetery increases the chances that one of them might have unresolved issues that would cause their spirit to roam.

One problem when looking at cemeteries and hauntings is confirmation bias: your mind naturally looks for evidence that supports your beliefs and ignores evidence to the contrary. Since most people believe cemeteries are haunted, they interpret experiences as a confirmation of that belief. That makes separating facts from fairy tales regarding cemetery ghosts difficult.

Logic would suggest that a person's spirit should have no connection to the cemetery since their body wasn't moved there until after the spirit had moved on (hopefully). However, if spirits can form a connection with a chair or with a house where they spent only part of their life, then it would seem that they would have the strongest connection with their bodies, with which they spent their entire lives.

LAUREL HILL CEMETERY
3822 RIDGE AVENUE

Laurel Hill is the second major rural cemetery in the United States. (The first is Mount Auburn in Boston, Massachusetts.) Founded in 1836, it sits on seventy-eight acres of land along the Schuylkill River. Before Laurel Hill was established, Philadelphians were either buried in churchyards or potter's fields. As churchyards filled up and became more expensive, Philadelphians became eager for an alternative. Laurel Hill became the place to be buried for socialites like Rittenhouse, Widener, Elkins, and Strawbridge. Forty Civil War–era generals are buried here—including General George Meade—as well as six *Titanic* passengers. Today, only one percent of the cemetery space is still available for burials.

Laurel Hill proudly embraces all of its dead, both those that remain under the ground and those who choose to walk above it. According to its website, they even offer private ghost hunts with paranormal investigators. Frank Cassidy, of the Free Spirit Paranormal Investigators, frequently leads ghost hunts at Laurel Hill. In his six years as an investigator, he has never called any place haunted, but he admits that some things at the cemetery can't be explained.

According to Cassidy, Section K has the most activity. Section K is located along Hunting Park Avenue next to the Schuylkill River. People frequently report feeling sick to their stomach in this area and the section has an overall creepy feeling to it. Shadowy figures in human form have been seen in here.

Another area with a lot of activity is Millionaire's Row, which is characterized by a curved road lined with mausoleums. As its nickname suggests, a number of wealthy Philadelphians have made this area their home, and they are particular as to how people should behave in their neighborhood. Whenever rowdy tours pass through this section, tour guides report feeling the ghosts pressing against them, urging them to hurry the crowd on. Shadowy shapes are also commonly reported here.

The most famous gravestone in Laurel Hill has to be the Schaaff Monument. Also known as the Crying Mother, this marble carving depicts a grieving mother holding two infants. Many folktales have been spread about it. Some say it overlooks the spot where a mother and her two children drowned on the river. Others say the children died in a boating accident and the grieving mother followed shortly after.

In reality, the woman buried beneath is Helena Schaaff, a renowned pianist who married Polish sculptor Henry Dmoghowski-Saunders in 1853. Tragically, their first child was stillborn on March 6, 1855. The second died during childbirth as did Helena on July 27, 1857. Henry buried the mother and two children together in Laurel Hill. He spent the next eighteen months carving the sculpture as a tribute to his lost family.

When he was finally finished, it is said he threw his tools in the Schuylkill River (although this was not his last sculpture) and returned to Poland. He was killed a few years later while leading a Polish uprising against Russian troops.

Helena may have made at least one ghostly appearance at Laurel Hill. An amateur photographer was taking photographs when she heard someone crying and saw a figure dash across her viewfinder. She lowered the camera to ascertain where the noise was coming from, when she saw her five-year-old son a step away from the Schuylkill River. Many people believe it was Helena's ghost stepping in to save the child from certain death.

In a 2014 interview, Cassidy expressed some skepticism about the story, since there is a one hundred foot drop between the monument and the river. It is not a place someone would allow a child to wander around without constant supervision.

Another story associated with the cemetery is that of Martha Drennan. Her father worked for the cemetery in the early 1900s, and she often spent time walking the grounds, until she went missing. According to a December 2, 1903, newspaper report, she had "left on Sunday [November 29] to go to New York." On March 10, 1904, a headless body was found in Delaware Bay. Two hours later, the body of an unidentified man was found in the same area. Although no relationship between the two was found, their proximity made authorities believe they were together when they went into the water.

Despite the fact that her body was found headless, it was determined Drennan had either fallen or jumped into the river. The authorities believed the ice had severed the head from its body. Newspaper reports stated it appeared the body had been in the water some time; however, the date of her death is listed as March 10, 1904, the date she was found. Identification was made by the woman's clothing and a ring she was wearing. She is currently buried in Section X of the cemetery, and her gravestone reads Martha Drinnan.

The mystery surrounding her death and her love for the cemetery make the odds of her spirit showing up a bit higher than others in the cemetery. Keep in mind when visiting the cemetery after dark that not every shadowy shape is supernatural. Deer and fox roam the cemetery, as do a number of homeless people.

PALMER CEMETERY
141 East Palmer Street

The Palmer Cemetery, also known as Kensington Burial Ground, is named after Anthony Palmer. Palmer donated the land for this cemetery with the hopes that residents could obtain a free plot. Ironically, he is not buried in this cemetery, because the cemetery hadn't been created yet. He is buried in Christ Church Burial Ground, although his exact plot is unknown. The cemetery has been in use since 1749. No one knows exactly how many people are buried here, but estimates have it in the tens of thousands.

Beyond the orbs and shadow people "running about" that are connected to most cemeteries, Palmer has two major ghosts. If you go to the cemetery at twilight, right after the streetlights turn on, you can see the ghost of a boy hanging from a "phantom branch" of a tree. The teenager committed suicide by the cemetery entrance from that very tree, although officials did cut down the branch he used.

According to online postings from a nearby resident, the suicide occurred on Easter Monday in 1995. And although he didn't mention which tree, a large tree by the Montgomery Street (at Miller Street) entrance that has a branch missing would fit the bill.

The other ghost (or ghosts) include a large white figure who stares through the fence while holding a baby. Reports only say the figure is "big" or "large" but don't explain if that means it is tall, wide, or both. (Technically, the baby would make three ghosts, but since it doesn't do anything but be held, it doesn't really count.)

Another unsubstantiated Internet rumor is that a visitor at Palmer Cemetery had placed flowers on a grave when they felt the strange feeling someone else was around. They turned to look, but didn't find anyone. When they turned back, the flowers were gone.

MOUNT MORIAH CEMETERY
6189 KESSINGTON AVENUE

In April 2002, the South Jersey Ghost Research investigated Mount Moriah Cemetery. One investigator reported seeing the figure of a man standing under a tree. But when he snapped a picture, an orb appeared where the man had been standing. The group caught a number of other orb pictures throughout the cemetery, as well.

Mount Moriah Cemetery was incorporated in 1855 and was closed in 2011. The last member of the Mount Moriah

Cemetery Association had died in 2004, which left the cemetery in a bizarre circumstance further complicated by the fact that the cemetery straddles both the city of Philadelphia and Yeadon. Luckily, a nonprofit organization called the "Friends of Mount Moriah" has stepped in to maintain the cemetery until an owner is decided—which is not easy, since it costs close to half a million dollars each year to maintain the cemetery.

CEDAR HILL CEMETERY/ NORTH CEDAR HILL CEMETERY/MOUNT CARMEL
FRANKFORD AND EAST CHELTENHAM AVENUES

Stand in the intersection of Frankford and East Cheltenham Avenues and you'll be surrounded by cemeteries. (Don't stand there for long or you'll risk ending up a resident and not a visitor of the cemeteries.)

Cedar Hill was established in 1850 on the northwest corner of Frankford and East Cheltenham Avenues. It later expanded to the other side of Frankford Avenue. North Cedar Hill Cemetery (technically Northeast of Cedar Hill) was added across East Cheltenham Avenue. In 1892, the Jewish cemetery Mt. Carmel was added on the last corner, resulting in all four corners of this intersection bordering a cemetery.

One of the most prominent features of Cedar Hill is a monument to Civil War soldiers. It lists the soldiers from Frankford who served in the war and is surrounded by the graves of thirty-three Civil War veterans. The monument also appears to be a gathering site for Civil War ghosts. Several people have reported seeing them gathering on the hill.

People also report hearing a "banshee" scream coming from the cemeteries, as well as a woman crying. It is unclear if one ghost or multiple ghosts make the noise, or in which of the three cemeteries the noise originates. Apparently, no one is brave enough to investigate screaming coming from a graveyard. One final ghost was described in June 2004 on the *Philadelphia Inquirer*'s Phillyblog as "a gray shadow floating along the cemetery wall."

TRINITY CHURCH, OXFORD, AND CEMETERY
6900 OXFORD AVENUE

Trinity Church, Oxford, also known as Old Trinity Church, is an Episcopal church that was originally founded in 1698. The church was built in 1711. In its 300-year history, the church building has expanded at least five times, and it is believed at least one of these expansions was built over a portion of the graveyard. The church supposedly used the headstones as part of the foundation without moving the bodies. The parish profile does mention at least five expansions to the original building, but not that any of them were over the graveyard.

A caretaker of the church reported in 1998 that he frequently heard footsteps and people talking when he was alone in the church. During an investigation, several members of the Philadelphia Ghost Hunters Alliance saw a figure walking past windows of the church and down the main aisle, heard tapping on the windows, and observed a doorknob moving, although they had been told no one was in the building. They felt it might be the spirit of a man who died in the church after falling from the bell tower.

Neighbors have seen the figure of a small girl sitting on the cemetery wall. She disappears before they can approach. Unlike some churches, Trinity doesn't reject the thought of its building and cemetery being haunted. They frequently host ghost tours through the cemetery and church.

FOREST HILLS CEMETERY
101 BYBERRY ROAD, HUNTINGDON VALLEY

A man dressed in a black tuxedo wanders through the tombstones of Forest Hills/Shalom Memorial Park. The Paranormal Investigators & Research Association of Philadelphia investigated the haunting. The name of the ghost has not been published because his wife and child are still alive. However, the man died in 1996, and his tombstone, where the apparition disappeared, has a picture embedded of him in a tuxedo. The cemetery is located just across the Philadelphia County line, in Montgomery County.

LEVERINGTON CEMETERY
6053 RIDGE AVENUE

Leverington Cemetery has been dubbed "the most actively documented location for orbs and apparitions in Philadelphia" as well as "a very haunted site" on the Internet. But information beyond that is elusive. The South Jersey Ghost Research organization investigated in 2006 and came back with pictures of orbs and of white mist. While the mist could be ectoplasm, it extends past the bottom of the picture, which makes it impossible to verify the picture's authenticity.

If Leverington is not haunted, it should be, considering its history and how it looks. The cemetery is surrounded by wrought iron fencing. Inside the cemetery you will find broken gravestones and overgrown brush obscuring the history buried here. Leverington Cemetery was originally the burial ground for the Levering family when Wigard Levering was buried there in 1745. Eventually it became part of the Roxborough Baptist Church, but in 1857 it severed its ties and became its own graveyard. Sadly, many of the cemetery records were destroyed in a fire in 1966.

ST. DOMINIC'S CATHOLIC SCHOOL
8500 FRANKFORD AVENUE

A number of websites and books say a "ghostly specter" roams the graveyard of St. Dominic's Catholic School. None of them explain why a Catholic school has a cemetery. In actuality, the cemetery (and school) belongs to the St. Dominic's Roman Catholic Church established in 1849. The large cemetery surrounds both the church and the school next door. According to Find-A-Grave.com, at least 4,300 people are buried here, with new ones being added.

Chapter 26

Former Burial Grounds

Most people shy away from disturbing a grave. The act is said to be sacrilegious. Disturbed graves are rumored to bring about curses and attract ghosts. However, love often trumps fear, and in Philadelphia some people love money more than they fear the possible consequences of disturbing someone's grave. At least, that's how it would appear, since an astounding number of burial grounds have been moved in Philadelphia.

In the 1700s and early 1800s, most Philadelphians were buried around churches. And since Philadelphia was known for its religious freedom, there were a lot of churches. If you couldn't afford a church burial, you were laid to rest in a potter's field. It wasn't until about the 1830s that cemeteries, burial grounds that included landscaping to create a park-like atmosphere, found their way to America. Laurel Hill, founded in 1836, was the first in Philadelphia and the second in the United States. As churchyards ran out of space, cemeteries sprang up in Philadelphia as a happy medium for those who might not be able to afford the churchyard burial but didn't want to be buried in an unmarked potter's grave.

As Philadelphia grew, however, land became more valuable and cemeteries that had been built in rural settings were now in urban settings. In some cases, upkeep in cemeteries became too expensive, especially if they were full, and nearly impossible when they were abandoned. In other cases, urban developers determined the land was too valuable to be "wasted" on a cemetery.

Moving a cemetery sounds like a difficult thing, and in the beginning it was. But lawmakers in Pennsylvania started making it easier. In 1891, a law was passed that allowed the purchase of burial grounds, provided the sellers used a portion of the money earned from the sale to remove the remains to a "suitable place for their re-interment."

As if that wasn't enough, in 1913 the Burial Grounds Conveyance Act allowed churches, cemeteries, and burial associations to disinter and reinter any remains, even if they were unable to contact the owner or caretaker of the lot, if a judge determined one of the following was true:

1. The burial ground is surrounded by improvements.
2. Keeping the bodies at that location would result in a public health danger.
3. The burial ground is neglected or a public nuisance.
4. The remains interfere with the "improvements, extension and general progressive interest of the Commonwealth or any city, borough, town or township."

Recently, laws have been passed that preserve older cemeteries by allowing them to be declared landmarks and allowing people to petition the city to step in to take care of abandoned or neglected cemeteries.

Funny thing about moving cemeteries—no one seemed to care how it was done. Once the claimed bodies were moved, the rest of the bodies were usually treated as nuisances. Although the laws were supposed to ensure that the graves were simply relocated, that didn't always happen.

Often instead of being reinterred in individual plots, the bodies were put in mass graves and the gravestones discarded. One such example, found in the March 27, 1886, *Philadelphia Inquirer,* stated that police "discovered a large number of human bones in a pit on Richmond Street." They determined that they were from the Zoar African Methodist Episcopal Church. Authorities forbade "any more bones being deposited in the pit, which was covered up with dirt."

There was no mention if the bones in the pit were removed. They may still be there, but at least some of the bodies were moved to Olive Cemetery (before being moved to Eden Cemetery after it closed). But the bodies were not always moved. On several occasions, bodies have been found on land that was once a cemetery in Philadelphia. A few examples:

- In November 1980, workers digging a subway tunnel unearthed the First African Baptist Church Cemetery.
- In 1999, graves from the United American Mechanics Cemetery were found after several houses were torn down.
- In June 2000, fifteen bodies from the Second Presbyterian Church Burial Ground were found when the city began work on the National Constitution Center.
- In 2009, the City of Philadelphia was working on building the Willard School over the former Franklin Recreation Center, which had been the Franklin Cemetery, when sound-penetrating radar tests on the ground discovered several intact burials.
- In July 2013, an archaeological investigation found "intact burial remains" a mere 2.5 feet below the

surface of Weccacoe Playground, formerly Mother Bethel Cemetery.

- In December 2013, workers at William Dick Elementary School found four coffins (complete with bodies) underneath the asphalt. The area had once belonged to Odd Fellows Cemetery.

Chapter 27
Digging Up the Dead

With so many moved graveyards, Philadelphia should be teeming with upset ghosts. Where are they? Well, a few of the sites do have recorded hauntings, but they are rarely mentioned. Other ghosts in Philadelphia simply have better press agents and the sites are limited to brief mentions in ghost books (if at all).

For example, the Saint Maria Goretti High School was built in the 1950s on land which used to be St. Mary's Cemetery. The only mention of it being haunted is in Katherine Driver's book *Philadelphia Haunts*. The book says that teachers and students report feeling cold hands touching them and seeing an unknown figure walking around the campus. The school, now known as Saints John Neumann-Maria Goretti High School, is located at 1736 South Tenth Street.

It's possible that the spirits are at peace with their disturbance, or perhaps no one has tried to make contact with them. Since a good portion of these are public areas like playgrounds and shopping centers, they seem ripe for a good paranormal investigation. But for the ones that are now residences, please respect the residents' privacy (and possibly their ignorance—they may not know that they live over a former cemetery!).

FORMER BURIAL GROUNDS IN PHILADELPHIA

Established in 1794, **African Episcopal Church of St. Thomas** used its cemetery until 1887, when the church was sold. Burials were relocated to Lebanon Cemetery in 1887 and then Eden Cemetery in 1903 after Lebanon closed. *Southwest corner of South Fifth Street and St. James Court*

All Saints Ground, or All Saints Episcopal Church or All Saints P.E., was established in 1838 and closed about 1915. At least twenty-five people were buried here in the 1850s and 1860s. It is unclear if the graves were moved before the church was sold in 1908 to a Greek Orthodox congregation, or if they remain. It is now the Rising Sun Baptist Church. On January 28, 1994, a five-alarm fire at this site took the lives of two firefighters, John Redmond and Vencent Acey. The church has since been rebuilt. *12th and Clymer Streets*

Arabella (Aribilla) Cemetery, or Beth Israel Cemetery, opened around 1844 and was moved to a mass grave in Roosevelt Memorial Park around 1935. Vare Washington Elementary School now sits here. *1198 South Fifth Street*

The **Arch Street Friends Burial Ground,** also known as Eastern Ground, is below the Friends Meeting House (known as the Arch Street Meeting House today) as the building was built over graves. The first recorded burial occurred in 1683. Some of the burials are currently located under Arch Street. Two smaller family burial grounds, Say and Jones, were located directly next to this land. Through the years some of the bodies have been excavated and reinterred at other cemeteries. *Arch and Fourth Streets*

Arch Street Second Presbyterian Churchyard, also called just the Second Presbyterian or Arch Street Churchyard, was built in 1743 on the northeast corner of Third and

Arch Streets. The 2,500 internments were moved to Mount Vernon Cemetery in 1867 when a new church was built (although some records say the church was demolished in 1837–1838). *Third and Arch Streets*

The **Arch Street Presbyterian Church**, formerly the Fifth Presbyterian, buried members at their church starting in 1822. The land was sold in 1903 and remains were moved to Arlington Cemetery in Delaware County. Several restaurants are currently located here. *South side of Arch Street between Tenth and Eleventh Streets*

The Old Asbury Methodist Episcopal Church was built in 1829 and included a burial ground called the **Asbury Cemetery**. However, when the church needed to expand in 1883, they moved the bodies to Mt. Moriah Cemetery and eventually demolished the old church. The area is now a parking lot next to the Marks Intercultural Center. *NW Corner of Chestnut and Thirty-Third Streets*

Bellevue (Belvue) Cemetery was established in 1885. It was moved in 1951 to Philadelphia Memorial Park in Frazer, Pennsylvania, for unknown reasons since the property lay abandoned until the 1960s. The Harrowgate Plaza Shopping Center lies on the property today. *North of Tioga Street between G Street and I Street*

Technically, **Mother Bethel Burial Ground** has not been moved—it's located under Weccacoe Playground. Weccacoe is a Lenape Indian word meaning "pleasant place," which is what most would call a playground on top of a cemetery. Bethel A.M.E. Church bought the land in 1810 for use as a private cemetery. It was used until 1864. The land was sold in 1888 to the city to fund a new church. In 1908, the city decided to make it into a playground, despite the fact that the 3,000 to 5,000 bodies were never moved. The graveyard is sometimes referred to as the Weccacoe Burial Ground. *400 block of Catharine Street*

Burials began at the **Blockley Baptist Church Grounds** in 1819 but finished in 1836. In June 1926, the location was excavated to a depth of one hundred feet and the more than one thousand bodies were removed. According to an article at the time, the site was then used for a series of church revivals. Burials were moved to West Chester and Mt. Zion Cemeteries. A tennis court is now located where the graves were. *SE corner of Fifty-Third Street and Wyalsuing Avenue*

In 1889, the area around east of Thirty-Third Street at South Street was purchased for use as a new Keystone Battery Armory. When they started digging the foundation, workers found three layers of human remains from **Blockley Almshouse Cemetery**, an old potter's field. The University of Pennsylvania took that opportunity to swoop in and purchase the land (for more money, too). It now lies underneath Franklin Field; more bodies were uncovered when it was constructed in the 1920s. Bodies were buried here between 1832 and 1860. *South of Thirty-Third and Spruce Streets*

A second **Blockley Almshouse Cemetery** was used between 1860 and 1905. In 2001, a parking garage was built here, which uncovered additional remains. Some were archaeologically exhumed and reburied in Woodlands Cemetery. The rest of the "dirt" (which likely contained human remains) was used as landfill beneath the FedEx Shipping Center in Gray's Ferry. *Civic Center Boulevard and South University Avenue*

An unnamed cemetery is located northeast of North and North Sixteenth Streets on ground that was once the country seat of Governor Andrew Hamilton. *The History of Philadelphia* mentions a Dr. Hurley purchasing land for a **Bush**

Hill Cemetery at Schuylkill Eighth (Fifteenth) Street below Coates (Fairmount) Avenue. It opened in 1836 and was used until 1853. City growth forced it to be moved. Remains were moved to St. Augustine's graveyard or Cathedral Cemetery if they were claimed. Unclaimed graves were moved to St. Dennis' Graveyard in Delaware County. A cemetery is listed near this location on the 1858-1860 atlas south of the Hedding Methodist Episcopal Church (now the Cavalry Baptist Church), so the cemetery could be associated with that church or with St. George's Methodist Episcopal Church, which purchased land for this use near here. *Northeast of North Sixteen and North Streets*

Ebenezer Methodist Episcopal Cemetery was closed in 1914. It was where the Southwark/Queen Village Community Garden is located. Hopefully, this is one of the cemeteries where they removed the bodies. *Christian Street between Third and Fourth Streets*

The **Epiphany Protestant Episcopal Church,** or Church of the Epiphany, stood for about seventy years on Fifteenth Street. Burials occurred here from 1838 until the 1860s. When it was sold in 1895, most of the remains were moved to West Laurel Hill Cemetery. *Northwest of Chestnut Street and South Fifteenth Streets*

Evangelical Lutheran Church of St. John, or St. John Evangelical Church, once stood where the Ben Franklin Bridge off-ramp is now located. The graves were moved in 1924 to Laurel Hill Cemetery. *Race Street between Fifth and Sixth Streets*

The **Fifth Baptist Church Burial Grounds** were used from 1825 until 1852. The remains were moved to Laurel Hill Cemetery. The land is currently a parking lot. *Southwest of Sansom and Eleventh Streets*

The **First African Baptist Church** burial ground actually refers to two different churches and cemeteries. The first church cemetery, or Tenth Street Cemetery, was used between 1810 and 1822. In 1983, it was discovered during the construction of I-676. Ninety sets of remains were exhumed between 1985 and 1990 and reinterred at Eden Cemetery. In 1816, the First African Baptist Church congregation divided. The second group established a church (and burial grounds) of the same name on the corner of Eighth and Vine Streets. This site is often referred to as the Eighth Street Cemetery for clarity and was used between 1823 and 1842. The Tenth Street Cemetery was discovered in 1980 during construction for a commuter rail tunnel. Nearly 150 people were exhumed from this site and reinterred in Eden Cemetery in 1987. *Tenth Street between Winter and Vine Streets and southwest corner of Eighth and Vine Streets*

First African Presbyterian Church was established in 1809. It moved to a new location around 1887 and moved the cemetery to Lebanon Cemetery. The location is now a coffeehouse. *Southeast corner of Bainbridge Street and South Seventh Street*

The **First Baptist Church** or Sansom Street Baptist Church was completed in 1763 complete with space in the graveyard to bury everyone who was a member for one dollar. The graveyard is indicated on the 1858–1860 atlas of the city but the land contained a felt hat factory by 1875. *Southwest corner of Arch Street and Little Boys Court*

First Moravian Burial Ground was established in 1757 and used until 1890. Remains were moved to Ivy Hill Cemetery. *Northwest corner of Vine and Franklin Streets*

A parking lot at the end of Lena Street now sits where **First Presbyterian Church Grounds** once did. Graves from this burial ground were moved to Ivy Hill or Laurel Hill Cemeteries. They also had land on Market Street that was used for burials. The remains from here were moved to a vault at Laurel Hill, while the tombstones were moved to Old Pine Street Church in the 1850s (although the website for Old Pine Street says graves were also moved here). *Between Haines and Center Street near Germantown Avenue and south side of Market Street between Bank and Strawberry Streets*

The **First Reform Church** established a church and cemetery here after being moved from their previous location on Franklin Square. Bodies moved from that site were reburied here along with some new ones. The property was sold in 1864 and remains were moved to Old Oaks Cemetery. But when that site didn't last, they were moved again (some for a third time) to West Laurel Hill in 1877. *Southeast of Cherry and North Seventeenth Streets*

The **First Reformed Presbyterian**, or Covenanters, was organized in 1798. It was sold to the Second African Presbyterian Church, who also used the burial grounds. The burying ground was sold in 1888 and transformed into Starr Garden Park. The church also used another site on Ludlow Street purchased in 1817. The land was sold in 1850 and remains moved, or that was the plan. When a theater erected on the site was demolished in 1911, a casket from 1825 was unearthed. A third First Reformed Presbyterian Church, complete with burial grounds, was located on Cherry Street near Eleventh in 1840. *North side of Rodman Street between Sixth and Seventh Streets and southeast corner of Eleventh and Ludlow Streets*

St. Josaphat's School and its parking lot now rest where the **Fourth Reformed Churchyard** once resided. The graves were moved to a common grave at Westminster Cemetery,

Bala Cynwy. *Grape Street midway between Silverwood and Cresson Streets*

Fourth Presbyterian Church purchased land on Lombard Street for burials. It was used until 1891, when the remains were moved to Mt. Moriah Cemetery. The site is now a series of row houses and a parking lot. *Southside of Lombard Street between Twelfth and Thirteenth Streets*

According to Philadelphia City Archives, at least thirty-five people were buried in the **Francisville Burial Grounds** between 1833 and 1834. The cemetery was sold in 1903 and the remains moved to Arlington Cemetery in Delaware County. *1700 block of Ridge Avenue*

Franklin Cemetery was established in 1840 and in use until 1921. In 1947, plans were made to move the eight thousand bodies to Evergreen Memorial Park and convert Franklin Cemetery to a playground. Records show $95,000 was paid to move about eight thousand bodies to three acres of Evergreen. In September 1988, construction work close to Evergreen revealed that the move had not gone as expected. First, Evergreen shows that they only received three thousand bodies, and no record existed of where the other five thousand bodies were sent. (For more information, see Lafayette Cemetery.) As if that wasn't enough, they didn't move all the bodies. In 2009, the land was converted to the Francis E. Willard Elementary School, at which time some unmoved graves were found. *Southeast of Ruth and East Orleans Streets*

Free Quakers Cemetery was first established in 1788. During the Civil War, unclaimed bodies of soldiers who died in the local military hospital were buried here. The bodies were moved in 1907 to Fatlands, Pennsylvania. *Southwest of Fifth and Locust Streets*

Two different **German Lutheran Cemeteries** once existed. The first was moved in the 1880s and is now the Old First Reformed Church of Christ. The graves were relocated to a new Lehigh Street location. In 1969, the graves were again reinterred in either a special section of the Philadelphia Memorial Park or in Greenmount Cemetery. Dr. Ethel Allen Elementary School currently sits where the second cemetery once was. *Southeast corner of Race and Fourth Streets and 3200 West Lehigh Avenue*

Germantown Potter's Field was lost until 2011 when a playground was being built next to the building and workers uncovered burials dating back to the 1760s. According to historical records, it was a cemetery for "strangers, negroes and mulattoes." The discovery delayed the demolition of the housing unit for two years until it could be confirmed that no human remains still remained under the building. Demolition finally occurred in 2014 and a new apartment highrise is expected to be completed in December 2015. *301 West Queen Lane*

Glenwood Cemetery took up several city blocks on Ridge Avenue near the railroad tracks. It was incorporated in 1851. Glenwood Avenue cuts through what used to be the cemetery. The remains were moved in 1938 to Glenwood Memorial Gardens. The former cemetery site is now a housing development seen on old maps as the James Wheldon Johnson Homes. *Ridge Avenue and Twenty-Seventh Street*

Hanover Street Burial Grounds included three separate graveyards once located inside its grounds: Kensington Methodist Episcopal Cemetery, Union Harmony Burial Grounds, and Union Wesleyan Church Cemetery. It was moved in 1922 (after the city condemned it) to Fernwood Cemetery, Forest Hills Memorial Park, or North Cedar Hill

Cemetery. The land is now the Isaac D. Hetzell Playground. *Thompson Street between Columbia and Earl Streets*

Kensington Union Cemetery has gone by several names, including Union Burial Ground of the Northern Liberties & Kensington, West Street Burial Ground, German Burial Ground, Union Burial Ground, Malt House Ground, and Thumlert Cemetery. It operated between 1831 and 1892. Its eastern border was on West Street, which is now Belgrade Street. It was moved to Northwood Cemetery and Palmer Cemetery. *Southwest corner of Gaul and East Berks Streets*

Lafayette Cemetery contained 47,000 bodies in 1946 when it was decided they should be moved to Evergreen Memorial Park in Bensalem. The hundred-year-old cemetery had fallen into disrepair and was condemned by the city. Thomas A. Morris was contracted to move the bodies to forty acres of the park where they would be reinterred and given new bronze markers. It wasn't until 1988 that the truth was uncovered: the bodies were dumped in thirty-two unmarked trenches. By the time it was discovered, it was far too late to do anything except leave the bodies buried where they were, with a simple plaque to mark the spot.

The former Lafayette Cemetery has been transformed into Capitolo Playground, but some of its former residents may have been missed (or refused to go). Ed Snyder tells of encountering a strange figure near the former graveyard on his blog The Cemetery Traveler. Snyder was eating at Geno's Steak when an elderly man sat near him. "His hair was slicked into an old style and his dark suit was way outdated," Snyder says on his blog. What is more shocking is the man was covered with dried blood. No one else at the restaurant seemed to notice the man as he sat there.

After about ten minutes, he got up. (Perhaps he decided to try Pat's King of Steak across the street. Only in Philly are two legendary cheesesteak places open twenty-four hours a day!) Only later, when Snyder realized how close he was to the former cemetery, did he consider that the elderly man may have "been one of the restless souls from what used to be called Lafayette Cemetery." *900 Federal Street*

Lebanon Cemetery began in 1849 and became one of the primary burial places for African Americans denied access to other cemeteries. But by 1899 it had become so run-down that it was condemned by the city. The land was purchased by the Eden Company in 1903 and the bodies were transferred to Eden Cemetery. At least a portion of the Steven Girard School lies on the former site of Lebanon Cemetery. *North side of Passyunk Avenue between Eighteenth and Nineteenth Streets*

Logan Family Graveyard was located inside Stenton Park. In 1891, Gustavus and Anna Logan deeded the property to the city of Philadelphia to protect the family graveyard located east of the house. The plan failed miserably, since in the 1950s the city paved over it without giving anyone any advance notice. (For more information about Anna Logan, see the Loudoun Mansion entry in chapter 18.) *Sixteenth and West Courtland Streets*

The **Lombard Street Central Presbyterian Church** was established around 1844. The congregation had built a series of brick burial vaults in the yard of the church, but it was assumed they were moved after the church left in 1939. However, in 2008 a front vault was discovered intact when the church was converted to a private residence. The remains were moved to Old Pine Presbyterian Church. *836 Lombard Street*

Around 1895, **Machpelah Cemetery** graves were moved to Graceland Cemetery (North Mount Moriah). It was founded in 1827. A CVS, Advance Auto, and Sherwin-Williams are now located here. *Washington Avenue between Tenth and Eleventh Streets*

Magdalen Asylum buried patients on their ground according to the Board of Health Registers. Burials occurred between 1838 and 1859. The land is now part of the Franklin Institute. *Northeast corner of Twenty-First and Race Streets.*

Monument Cemetery was once located between Broad Street and Seventeenth Street and between Norris and Montgomery. For more information about this cemetery, see "Betsy Ross Bridge" in chapter 2.

Monumental Baptist Church was also known as Oak Street Baptist Church. In April 1884, the church relocated burials from the churchyard to Olive Cemetery so they could construct a new church building. The congregation remained at this location until 1962. The church building, which was painted bright red around 2008, remains. *4101 Ludlow Street*

The first cemetery in Philadelphia was the **Mutual Family Burying Ground**, established in 1826. It is listed as "Union Burying Ground" by G.W. Bromley on his 1895 and 1910 atlases of the city. The land is now a strip mall. Graves were moved in 1924 to Forrest Hills Cemetery. *Southeast corner of Washington Avenue and Tenth Street*

Ninth Presbyterian Church was located on the corner of Nineteenth and Race Streets until the land was sold and the Academy of Natural Sciences was built here. The cemetery connected with the church remained, however, although burials on the plot were prohibited after 1833. Efforts to move the cemetery in the mid-1800s were prevented because relatives objected. Finally, after a legal battle, the forty-two bodies were moved in the 1860s to Mt. Moriah Cemetery.

According to a newspaper article at the time, the cemetery was believed to be haunted. One of the tombstones that belonged to a young woman had the words "Gone but not Forgotten" written on it. The words were not in the same lettering as the names and dates. According to legend, the words were carved by a jilted lover of the girl. She had refused to marry him before she had died. Shortly after her death, he crept into the graveyard, carved those words on her tomb, and then committed suicide Romeo and Juliet style: he drank poison on her tomb. Locals believed his ghost haunted the cemetery. No one knows if his ghost still haunts the site or if he moved with his beloved's grave. *Southwest corner of Nineteenth and Race Streets*

Established in 1849, **Odd Fellows Cemetery** was a very large cemetery that sat between the railroad tracks and Twenty-Second Street. United American Mechanics Cemetery, which sold lots to Order of American Mechanic members, was part of Odd Fellows. The City of Philadelphia took it over in 1951 and built the Raymond Rosen Housing Development. Graves were moved to Lawnview Cemetery and Mount Peace Cemetery. *Diamond Street between Norris and Dauphin*

Old Oaks Cemetery was established in 1868–1869. At least some burials occurred here, but by 1884 the cemetery had been abandoned. What happened after that is unclear, but it seems that some of the burials were moved to West Laurel Hill. *Southwest of West Hunting Park and Wissahickon Avenues*

Olive Cemetery was an African American graveyard established in 1849 and moved in 1923 to Eden Cemetery. The Stephen Smith Home Burial Ground was also located here. The Blankenburg Elementary School and Stephen Smith Towers Apartments are now located here. *Girard Avenue between Merion and Belmont*

Philadelphia Cemetery was often referred to as New Philadelphia Cemetery to distinguish it from Ronaldson Cemetery. It was opened in 1828 and used until 1902. Bodies were moved to Arlington Cemetery in Drexel Hill around 1915. *Passyunk Avenue between Twentieth and Twenty-Second Streets.*

Philanthropic Cemetery existed between 1842 and 1874. A series of row houses are now at its former location. Graves were moved to Arlington Cemetery. *Northeast of Tasker and Twelfth Streets*

Ronaldson Cemetery, also known as Philadelphia Cemetery, was the model burying place in the city after it was founded in the 1820s, mainly because James Ronaldson spent quite a bit of money on it. It was moved in the 1950s by Thomas A. Morris. He was supposed to rebury the 13,500 bodies in individual plots with aluminum markers in Forest Hills Cemetery. Instead he buried them in a mass grave with a single marble spire to indicate where they are, similar to what he did with Lafayette and Franklin Cemeteries. The land is now Palumbo Playground. *South of Bainbridge Street between Ninth and Tenth Streets*

Rose Burying Ground was moved sometime between 1895 and 1910. Interestingly, the trapezoid-shape building that currently sits here is the exact shape of the original Rose Burying Ground. *4050 Ludlow Street*

When **St. John's Episcopal Church** decided to expand their church, they decided rather to build over the graves. They did move the stones, which are leaning against the building. (This may sound callous, but many churches feel it is better not to disturb the buried and some companies specialize in putting in foundation around dead bodies.) The church is now the Holy Trinity Romanian Orthodox Church. *222 Brown Street*

St. Joseph's Roman Catholic Cemetery was also known as Bishop's Burial Ground. Established in 1824, graves from Old St. Joseph's small cemetery were transferred here. The property was part of a lengthy legal battle in the late 1800s, during which the cemetery closed. In 1905 the property was sold and bodies not claimed by relatives were buried in Holy Cross Cemetery. On an old atlas, the German Roman Catholic Holy Trinity is listed as adjoining this cemetery. *North of Washington Avenue between Eighth Street and East Passyunk Avenue*

Two cemeteries associated with **St. Mary's Church** (located at Fourth and Spruce Streets) have been moved. The first was located on Thirteenth Street where the University of the Arts is currently located. It was sold in May 1899 and the bodies were moved to another cemetery on Eleventh Street. In 1956, that cemetery was moved to a mass grave at Holy Cross Cemetery in Yeadon and the St. Maria Goretti High School for Girls was put in its place. Apparently, the cemetery's residents got tired of all the moving, and the school is rumored to be haunted. *Southeast of Cypress and Juniper Streets and northeast of Moore and South Eleventh Streets*

St. Michael's Evangelical Lutheran Church was located where the Philadelphia Mint now sits. It was used from 1748 until 1875. Remains were moved to Lutheran Cemetery on Hart's Lane. *North of Fifth and Arch Streets*

St. Paul's Protestant Episcopal Church purchased ground in the early 1800s for use as a cemetery, known as **St. Paul's**

Cemetery. However, in 1859 an act of Assembly forced them to move remains buried here to Mount Moriah Cemetery, and the land around the church was sold. *Northeast of Third Street and St. James Place*

St. Stephen's Church Graveyard was moved before 1875. Its former location is under the Pennsylvania Convention Center. *East of Cherry and 13th Streets*

Scots Presbyterian Burial Ground was built in the late 1770s. The land was sold in 1889 and is now a series of row houses. *South side of Spruce Street between Third and Fourth Streets*

Second Presbyterian Church buried bodies on Arch Street between 1750 and 1804. They sold the land in 1868. According to records, 1,479 bodies were moved to Mt. Vernon Cemetery. They missed a few bodies that weren't discovered until 2000 during preparations to build the National Constitution Center. *Northwest corner of Arch and Fifth Streets*

Spruce Street Baptist used the land behind their church as a burial ground in the 1800s. The remains were moved in 1910. The church is currently the Society Hill Synagogue. *418 Spruce Street*

Trinity Episcopal Church Burial Ground became the Mario Lanza Park after those interred here were moved to Mount Moriah Park. *Queen Street between Second and Third Streets*

Union Baptist Church was located on Little Pine (Addison) Street from 1848 until 1888. When the founding pastor of this congregation died in 1850, he was buried in this cemetery. In 1888, the church was granted permission from the Board of Health to relocate burials, but something happened and this was never completed. Over a hundred years later in the late 1990s, remains from the cemetery were uncovered during construction of a private residence. The home owner and descendants of the congregation discussed relocating the cemetery, but nothing happened. A Union Methodist Church about a half block away on Sixth Street may also have had a cemetery, so it is highly likely that the cemetery remains buried underneath the south side of Addison Street. *Addison Street between Sixth and Seventh Streets*

Union Burial Ground, also called Sixth Street Union Cemetery and Union Sixth Street Cemetery, was incorporated in 1841 and catered to poorer members of Philadelphia. It should not be confused with the Union Burial Ground located at Tenth Street and Washington Avenue. By the 1960s, the cemetery was abandoned and frequently targeted by vandals. It was sold in 1970 and the bodies were moved to Philadelphia Memorial Park. *Both sides of Sixth Street between Washington Avenue and Federal Street*

The St. David's Society purchased land on Market Street that extended to Oak Street (now Ludlow) in 1809 as a burial ground for its members. Ownership was conveyed to the Welsh Society in 1834 and it became known as the **Welsh Burying Ground.** In 1864, the bodies were removed to Mount Moriah cemetery. The land is now used for a garage and public school. *4040 Market Street*

Wesley AME Zion Church was established in 1862. In 1885, the church was granted permission to relocate burials in its churchyard to Olive Cemetery. Today, the church is the Historic Congregation B'nai Abraham Synagogue. *527 Lombard Street*

Western Burial Ground was also known as the Friends Western Burial Ground and Sassafras Burial Ground. Burials occurred here between 1823 up until 1864. In 1915, construction of the parkway at Seventeenth and Cherry resulted in several graves being moved to Marshall Road Burial Ground. Then in 1922, a new building at Friends Select forced the removal of additional bodies. Some were reinterred on the site, while others were moved to other cemeteries. Today, the Friends Select School, a rental car office, and Strayer University occupy the former burial grounds. *Race Street between Sixteenth and Seventeenth Streets*

The **Wharton Street Methodist Episcopal Church** used to have a burial ground on Wharton Street. The church moved in 1907. It is unclear when the cemetery was closed, but at least one thousand of the bodies that formerly rested here now lay in Mount Moriah Cemetery. It is now St. Casimir's Catholic Church. *324 Wharton Street*

In 1797, the city converted the Wigwam tavern for use as a hospital. Land around the **"Wigwam" Hospital** was used for burials until it was filled to capacity in 1805. There is no indication that the burial ground was moved. Most likely it was either destroyed by development or still lays somewhere underneath it. *Foot of Race Street near the east bank of the Schuylkill River*

The Mother African Zoar Methodist Episcopal Church was once located on Brown Street and included the **Zoar African Methodist Burial Ground**. In 1884, the church received permission from the Board of Health to relocate burials in the churchyard to Olive Cemetery. Things didn't go as planned, however, because articles in the *Philadelphia Inquirer* in 1886 reported that the police found bones from the churchyard in a pit on Richmond Street near Clearfield. Orders were issued forbidding any more remains being put in the pit, which was then covered up with dirt. Whether those remains were ever moved is unclear, although some remains were relocated to Olive Cemetery.

Northwest of Brown and Fourth Streets and Richmond Street near Clearfield Street

A burial ground used by **Zion Evangelical Lutheran** existed from the mid-1770s until about 1865. According to an October 22, 1867, article in the Public Ledger, removal of bodies occurred for several days and digging for the cellars for stores to be erected on the site had begun. The article also says that "unless the friends of those buried in the ground desire it, no bodies will be removed from the ground except such as lie within a hundred and ten feet from the west wall, the space occupied by the new buildings." So there is a good chance that many of the bodies never got moved. Those that were moved were reinterred at German Lutheran Cemetery on Lehigh Avenue. The Metro Club Condo Association is currently located here. *North of Race Street between Franklin and Eighth Streets*

POTTER'S FIELDS

Philadelphia had several city potter's fields over the years where they buried people who couldn't afford a church burial or those whose bodies were unclaimed. These fields were used, according to one city ordinance, "as a place for interment of the bodies of deceased strangers and persons not members of any religious society at the time of their decease." For clarity, these places are listed by location unless a clear name is connected to them.

- The city municipal hospital had a potter's field, known as Hart's Lane Burying Ground, southwest of Lehigh and Nineteenth Streets that was in use from 1855 until 1908. Interestingly, on the 1862 atlas by Samuel L. Smedley it is listed as "City Greenhouse and Burial Ground." (Wonder what they used as fertilizer . . .)

Some of the graves were exhumed between 1908 and 1909 and cremated on the site. It is unclear what was done with the remains.

- Another **potter's field** opened in 1914 on the southwest corner of East Luzerne Street and Whitaker Avenue. Bodies were buried for a year and a day, and then cremated at the Philadelphia Municipal Hospital next door. At least, they were until the crematorium broke. After that, bodies piled up and caused a political scandal during the 1955 mayoral race. Today, the land is used as a police parking lot.

- Two separate **public burial grounds** were established on the south side of Lombard Street. The first, between Tenth and Twelfth Streets, was established in 1787 to use for the "interment of strangers and others." By 1800, this land was completely full and was sold in the 1850s. At least part of this land is now the Friends of Seger Park Playground. The second public burial ground was established down the block between Ninth and Tenth in 1800 but was no longer used after 1816. It may have been left intact.

- **Cherry Hill Burial Ground** was a potter's field first used in 1793 and may have been where Bush Hill Hospital buried yellow fever patients during the 1793 outbreak. Other city hospitals also used it in the early 1800s for patients of contagious diseases. The current status of the cemetery is unknown (it may have been moved or it may still be intact). *South side of Fairmount between Nineteenth and Twentieth Streets*

- Another **municipal burial ground** that was established in 1790 and abandoned in 1856 existed on the south side of Vine Street between Twenty-First and Twenty-Second Streets. However, it's possible no burials may have occurred there.

- Part of Logan's Square was used for public burials starting in 1812. It was located on the east side. In 1890, a plumber came across a coffin while excavating on Nineteenth Street for a drain pipe. Then in 2009, archaeologists discovered at least sixty intact graves at Sister Cities Park. The graves were not exhumed, but left undisturbed.

- Two potter's fields were located north of Market Street west of Schuylkill River in the early 1800s. Smedley's 1862 atlas lists an "Old Graveyard" on both sides of Bridgewater (now Thirtieth Street), which matches the location (north of Market Street near the river) listed in the *History of Philadelphia: 1609-1884*. They were known as **Lower Burying Ground** and **Upper Burying Ground**. They were likely destroyed in the mid-1800s by the Pennsylvania Railroad.

- In 1816, the city decided to establish a new potter's field outside the city limits, which would allow them to close their current ones and prohibit burials in public squares. They established the **Burying Ground at the Vineyard**. Its original location was the northeast corner of George and Charles Streets, which means that present-day Twentieth and Parish Streets both go through this ground. It was used between 1818 and 1860. The graves were moved by the city in 1861— at least that's what everyone believed. However in 1890 and in 1895, workers discovered remains under Twentieth Street. Then in 2009, seven more graves were discovered during repairs to a house on the 800 block of Twentieth Street.

- The Moyamensing Potter's Field was established on Tidmarsh (now Carpenter) Street between Eleventh and Twelfth Streets in 1822. It has been referred to as the Moyamensing Potter's Field and the Philadelphia Almshouse Burial Ground. It was used until 1850 and plainly never moved. In 1851, graves were uncovered at Twelfth and Carpenter. Then in 1898, several additional graves were found at Twelfth and Kimball. In 2004, renovations in the basement of a building on the south side of Carpenter uncovered the coffins (and well-preserved remains) of sixteen infants and seven adults. This suggests that the cemetery was never moved. However, the *Annals of Philadelphia* and *History of Philadelphia* state that the graveyard was located *north* of Tidmarsh, and Kimball is south of it. However, this could be a burial ground associated with the Philadelphia Almshouse, which is sometimes listed as part of Moyamensing and is said to have extended as far south as Washington Avenue.

- The Moyamensing Almshouse Burial Ground was used between 1816 and 1850. Its exact location is unclear, but it is somewhere between Fifteenth and Sixteenth Streets south of Fitzwater Street. In 1893, repairs to a building at 754 South Sixteenth Street uncovered forty-five intact coffins. The remains were removed to an undisclosed location.

BIBLIOGRAPHY

Writing this book required me to access a number of sources, too many to list here. Instead I included sources that I felt would be good starting points for anyone who wishes to learn more about Philadelphia and its ghosts.

Books

Adams, Charles J. *Philadelphia Ghost Stories*. Reading, PA: Exeter House Books, 1998.

Barefoot, Daniel W. *Spirits of '76: Ghost Stories of the American Revolution*. Winston-Salem, NC: John F. Blair, Publisher, 2009.

Bracelin, Cynthia. *Philadelphia's Haunted Historic Walking Tour*. Atglen, PA: Schiffer Publishing, 2008.

Coulombe, Charles A. *Haunted Places in America*. Guilford, CT: Lyons Press, 2004.

Diehl, Daniel, and Mark Donnelly. *Haunted Houses: Guide to Spooky, Creepy, and Strange Places across the USA*. Mechanicsburg, PA: Stackpole Books, 2010.

Eberlein, Harold Donaldson, and Horace Mather Lippincott. *The Colonial Homes of Philadelphia and Its Neighbourhood,*. Philadelphia and London: J.B. Lippincott, 1912.

Federal Writers' Project. *Pennsylvania: A Guide to the Keystone State*. New York: Oxford University Press, 1940.

Graham, George R. *Graham's American Monthly Magazine of Literature, Art, and Fashion*. Vol. 18–19. Philadelphia: G. R. Graham [etc.], 1841.

Hull, Laurie. *Philly's Main Line Haunts*. Atglen, PA: Schiffer Publishing, 2009.

Lake, Matthew, and Mark Sceurman. *Weird Pennsylvania: Your Travel Guide to Pennsylvania's Local Legends and Best Kept Secrets*. New York: Sterling Publishing, 2005.

Guiley, Rosemary. *Ghosthunting Pennsylvania*. Cincinnati, Ohio: Clerisy Press, 2009.

Harland, Marion. *Colonial Homesteads and Their Stories*. Vol. 1–2. New York: G.P. Putnam's Sons, 1912.

Hoffman, Elizabeth P. *In Search of Ghosts: Haunted Places in the Delaware Valley*. Philadelphia: Camino Books, 1992.

Hull, Laurie. *Brandywine Valley Ghosts: Haunts of Southeastern Pennsylvania*. Atglen, PA: Schiffer Publishing, 2008.

Jeffery, Adi-Kent Thomas. *Ghosts in the Valley; [True Hauntings in the Delaware Valley]*. Washington, DC: Rowe Publishing, 1971.

Jellett, Edwin Costley. *Germantown Gardens and Gardeners*. Germantown, Philadelphia: H.F. McCann, 1914.

Keith, Charles Penrose. *Chronicles of Pennsylvania from the English Revolution to the Peace of Aix-la-Chapelle, 1688–1748*. Philadelphia: Patterson & White, 1917.

Nesbitt, Mark, and Patty A. Wilson. *The Big Book of Pennsylvania Ghost Stories*. Mechanicsburg, PA: Stackpole Books, 2008.

Nesbitt, Mark, and Patty A. Wilson. *Haunted Pennsylvania: Ghosts and Strange Phenomena of the Keystone State*. Mechanicsburg, PA: Stackpole Books, 2006.

Norman, Michael, and Beth Scott. *Historic Haunted America*. New York: TOR, 1995.

Reeser, Tim. *Ghost Stories of Philadelphia, PA*. 1st Sight Press, 2007.

Riccio, Dolores, and Joan Bingham. *Haunted Houses USA*. New York: Pocket Books, 1989.

Rule, Leslie. *Ghosts Among Us: True Stories of Spirit Encounters*. Kansas City, MO: Andrew McMeel, 2004.

Sarro, Katharine. *Philadelphia Haunts at Eastern State Penitentiary, Fort Mifflin, & Other Ghostly Sites*. Atglen, PA: Schiffer Publishing, 2008.

Watson, John F. *Annals of Philadelphia: Being a Collection of Memoirs, Anecdotes, and Incidents of the City and Its Inhabitants, from the Days of the Pilgrim Founders . . . to Which Is Added an Appendix, Containing Olden Time Researches and Reminiscences of New York City*. Philadelphia: E.L. Carey & A. Hart, 1830.

Articles

Avery, Ron. "At Mansion, A Spirit of Renewal Did Ghosts Watch Over Treasures?" Philly.com. January 17, 1994. http://articles.philly.com/1994-01-17/news/25824934_1_treasures-smoke-and-water-damage-fire.

Blanchard, Matthew P. "The Rabbi and Mad Anthony Wayne." Philly.com. May 10, 2004. http://articles.philly.com/2004-05-10/news/25382367_1_jewish-life-yarmulkes-aish-hatorah.

Brooks, Emily. "Top 6 Haunted and Eerie Spots in Northwest Philly." Newsworks.org. October 30, 2013. www.newsworks.org/index.php/local/nw-philadelphia/61355-top-6-haunted-and-eerie-spots-in-northwest-philly.

Ernst, Katherine. "Philadelphia's Most Haunted Places." CBS Philly. October 12, 2012. http://philadelphia.cbslocal.com/top-lists/philadelphias-most-haunted-places/.

Gerhart, Ann. "Stalking City's Ghosts Guided Tour of Spirit Stomping Grounds." Philly.com. October

28, 1994. http://articles.philly.com/1994-10-28/
news/25874559_1_friendly-ghost-top-hat-dark-street.
"Most Haunted Attractions In and Around Philadelphia."
www.visitphilly.com/articles/philadelphia/most-
haunted-attractions-in-and-around-philadelphia/.

Mrykalo, Larissa. "Paranormal Pop Culture: Haunted Hot
Spots of Philadelphia, Pennsylvania." Paranormal Pop
Culture: Haunted Hot Spots of Philadelphia, Pennsylvania. www.paranormalpopculture.com/2014/06/haunted
-hot-spots-of-philadelphia.html.

Mucha, Peter. "Scaring up a Better List of Philly's 'Ghosts'"
Philly.com. October 13, 2011. http://articles.philly
.com/2011-10-13/news/30275571_1_ghost-hunters-
legends-and-ghost-stories-syfy.

Read, Madlen. "Perspective: Haunted Philadelphia." The
Daily Pennsylvanian. October 29, 2005. www.thedp.com/
article/2002/10/perspective_haunted_philadelphia.

Shapiro, Howard. "Benjamin Franklin, Still Cashing in
The Pennies Pile up on His Grave." Philly.com. November 2, 2004. http://articles.philly.com/2004-11-02/
news/25379094_1_pennies-ben-franklin-christ-church-
burial-ground.

Snyder, Susan. "Ghost Legends Thrive at Philadelphia-area
Colleges." Philadelphia Inquirer, October 31, 2009.

Thomas, Brittany. "Uwishunu's Guide to Experiencing
Haunted Philadelphia." October 17, 2012. www.uwis-
hunu.com/2012/10/uwishunus-guide-to-experiencing-
haunted-philadelphia/.

Volk, Steve. "An Old City Haunt." Philadelphia Weekly.
February 8, 2006. Accessed November 12, 2014. www
.philadelphiaweekly.com/news-and-opinion/an_old_
city_haunt-38411544.html.

Wink, Christopher. "The Supernatural: Graves and Ghosts at Temple." *The Temple News*. October 30, 2007. http://temple-news.com/opinion/the-supernatural-graves-and-ghosts-at-temple/.

Websites
Ghost Stories: paranormalstories.blogspot.com/2011/03/uss-olympia.html
Greater Philadelphia GeoHistory Network: www.philageohistory.org/geohistory/
Haunted Houses.com: www.hauntedhouses.com/
The Haunted Internet: www.thehauntedinternet.com/
Haunted Places.org: www.hauntedplaces.org/
Pennsylvania Haunts & History: hauntsandhistory.blogspot.com/
PhillyHistory.org: www.phillyhistory.org
South Jersey Ghost Research: www.southjerseyghostresearch.org/
StrangeUSA.com: www.strangeusa.com/
Tri County Paranormal Research: www.delcoghosts.com/index.html
Unexplainable.net: www.unexplainable.net/

GHOSTLY GLOSSARY

Anomaly: An event that is out of place and can't be explained by science or other logic.

Apparition: The appearance of a ghost or spirit using one of the senses. Visual apparitions can be found at most locations mentioned in this book, including Leah's ghost at Washington Square and Captain McPherson's ghost at Mount Pleasant. An example of an auditory apparition is the sound of footsteps heard at Carpenter's Hall. The smell of lemons at Lemon Hill Mansion is an example of an olfactory apparition. Women have experienced a tactile apparition at General Wayne Inn when a ghost blew on the back of their necks.

Apport: A physical object that materializes at will, supposedly caused by a spirit attempting to make its presence known. Coins at Ben Franklin's grave are an example of an apport.

Clearing or Cleansing: A ritual designed to rid a location of paranormal activity. Smudging, which uses incense to purify an area, is one method of cleansing.

Cold Spot: A self-contained area where the temperature is several degrees lower than the area around it. These spots are believed to be areas where a ghost is attempting to materialize. As a result, they are absorbing the heat around them. Cold spots are frequently found at Independence Hall, Old Pine Street Church, and the Civil War & Underground Railroad Museum of Philadelphia.

Collective Apparition: An instance where multiple people experience paranormal activity, either simultaneously or independently. In the 1880s, a collective apparition occurred at St. Peter's Churchyard.

Crisis Apparition: An apparition seen by someone who later discovers that the subject has died. The appearance of Justinia to the Wister girls at Grumblethorpe is an example of a crisis apparition.

Dowsing: Using rods or a pendulum to obtain information. They have been used to look for lost items, search for water underground, find missing people, and communicate with ghosts.

Earthbound: A term used to refer to spirits who are unable to cross over after death. Ghosts may be earthbound because they have unresolved issues or because they are afraid to cross over.

Ectoplasm or Ectoplasmic Mist: Originally, it was a fog-like substance exuded from mediums communicating with the spirit world. Today, it is used to describe any cloudy mist believed to be produced by ghosts. Amelia at Baleroy Mansion frequently appeared as a blue ectoplasmic mist.

Electromagnetic Field (EMF): A field containing both magnetic and electrical properties that surrounds an object with an electrical charge. High EMF levels can cause health problems including nausea, headaches, fatigue, paranoia, hallucinations, anxiety, feeling vibrations, and insomnia. Some devices known for producing high EMF levels are electric clocks, electric blankets, computers, fluorescent lamps, microwave ovens, and televisions.

Electromagnetic Field Meter: Better known as an EMF meter, this device detects the level of electro-magnetic field in milliGauss (mG). EMF meters are used in paranormal investigations in two different ways. The first is to get a baseline EMF level and detect any areas that have high EMF levels that are caused by electronic devices. The second is to detect any distortions or changes that occur in the normal electromagnetic field that might be due to paranormal activity. Houses usually have EMF levels between 0.2 and 1 mG.

Electronic Voice Phenomenon (EVP): The recording of ghostly voices or sounds on a recording device. Often, nothing can be heard at the time the tape was recording, but the ghostly voices or sounds can be heard when the recording is later played back.

Entity: An intelligent ghost that attempts to connect with the living.

Epicenter: A person or persons that is the focus of a poltergeist or haunting. Blonde women could be considered epicenters in Casemate 4 of Fort Mifflin since paranormal activity seems to increase when they are around.

Exorcism: A religious ritual, usually done by a priest or demonologist, used to rid a location or person of evil spirits. It is considered a stronger method than a cleansing.

Ghost Hunt/Paranormal Investigation: An investigation at a location believed to be haunted. These take many different forms from informal, casual observation to carefully controlled research projects.

Ghost Hunter: A person who investigates areas suspected to be haunted. Ghost hunters may use scientific methods and equipment or psychic impressions.

Ghost Lights: Mysterious lights seen at a distance. They may appear as blue or yellow spheres or appear to blink, like a candle flame. The lights on the grounds of Loudoun Mansion are an example of ghost lights. Also known as "Will-o'-the-wisp," ignis fatuus, and a variety of other terms.

Gray Lady: The ghost of a woman whose death is connected to her lover, either by murder or suicide. The name is given to a number of ghosts, including the one that haunted Chalkley Hall. In the Harry Potter series, Helena Ravenclaw was nicknamed the Grey Lady. (In America, the term is spelled g-r-A-y; in England it is spelled g-r-E-y.)

Hot Spot: A specific area within a haunted location where high levels of paranormal activity are recorded.

Imprint: See Residual Hauntings.

Manifestation: Tangible signs that a location is haunted, usually measured during an investigation. (*See also* Apparition.)

Medium: A person who claims to be able to communicate with the dead.

Mist: A photographed anomaly usually not seen by the naked eye that appears as a cloud or haze. Although some believe this is caused by ectoplasm, environmental causes such as a reflection or moisture must be ruled out.

Occam's Razor: The principle that one should always look to the simplest or most logical explanation for an event, usually expressed as "When you hear hoofbeats, think horses and not zebras." This cautions people not to always assume that an event is caused by ghosts, but to eliminate other possible sources of the phenomenon.

Orb: A sphere of light caught on film. These can vary in size, color, and density. Some believe that orbs are spirits or ghosts. However, a camera flash can reflect off small objects and cause orbs. Dust, rain, and insects are common natural causes of orbs.

Ouija Board: A board printed with letters, numbers, and words which uses a planchette to communicate with the dead. Although it is currently sold as a "board game," caution should be used before attempting to use one.

Paranormal: Any experience that is above or outside the natural order of things. Ghosts, UFOs, and ESP are all considered part of the paranormal.

Parapsychology: A field of study that focuses on paranormal and psychic phenomenon.

Phantom Animals: Animals who appear as ghosts. The cat at Bishop White's house is an example of a phantom animal.

Poltergeist: A German word that means "noisy or rowdy ghost." The term is often used to describe a ghost that frequently interacts with the physical world. Steven at Baleroy Mansion is an example of a poltergeist.

Portal: A theory that locations may have doorways of energy that allow spirts to enter and exit the physical world.

Psychic: A person with above-average extrasensory perception. Psychics are believed to be able to gain information using their subconscious and be more sensitive to paranormal phenomenon than others.

Reciprocal Apparition: An experience in which a ghost and a living person react to each other.

Residual Hauntings: Ghostly activity that appears to be unconscious and repetitious. These hauntings are believed to be caused when the energy of an event is recorded or imprinted onto a location and then replayed whenever the conditions are right. These ghosts do not interact with those around them. The ghosts at the Merchant Exchange are an example of a residual haunting. Also referred to as imprint hauntings, energy hauntings, or atmospheric apparitions.

Séance: A group of people who sit in a circle and attempt to communicate with the dead. The event is usually conducted by a medium.

Sensitive: A person who is able to feel the presence of paranormal energy. They are also called empaths.

Shadow Ghosts or Figures: A ghost that appears as a dark shape. Shadow ghosts are usually darker than normal shadows and impervious to light. They appear in a variety of shapes, from human forms to cloud-like outlines.

Skeptic: A person who believes that paranormal activity can be explained using rational or scientific means.

Spiritualism: A belief that the spiritual world is able to communicate with the living.

Supernatural: Something that occurs through a means other than that known in nature. Similar to paranormal, "supernatural" usually refers to events with a divine or demonic nature.

Vortex: A small funnel- or tornado-shaped image that appears in photographs.

INDEX

ABOUT THE AUTHOR

Darcy Oordt grew up in a ghostly desert: There is not one known haunted house in her hometown of Blue Earth, Minnesota. It wasn't until she moved to Tennessee that she experienced her first ghost, while working as a tour guide for a "ghost" tour. Her first book, *Finding Success After Failure: Inspirational Stories of Famous People Who Persevered and Won Out,* tells about the early failures of famous people and how they overcame them.

In her free time, Darcy enjoys swimming with sharks, flipping houses, and exploring museums in exotic locations . . . if by "enjoy" you mean watching it on television. When she is not writing, you will usually find her making jewelry or crafts, fussing with one of her freshwater aquariums, or spending time with her pets.

Darcy currently lives near Cherry Hill, New Jersey, across the bridge from the many phantoms of Philadelphia.